HARCOURT SOCIAL Studies

Regions Around Us

Harcourt

SCHOOL PUBLISHERS

www.harcourtschool.com

HARCOURT SOCIAL Studies

Regions Around Us

Series Authors

Dr. Michael J. Berson
Professor
Social Science Education
University of South Florida
Tampa, Florida

Dr. Tyrone C. Howard
Associate Professor
UCLA Graduate School of Education &
   Information Studies
University of California Los Angeles
Los Angeles, California

Dr. Cinthia Salinas
Assistant Professor
Department of Curriculum and
   Instruction
College of Education
The University of Texas at Austin
Austin, Texas

North Carolina Consultants and Reviewers

Jenny Bajorek
Teacher
Northwoods Elementary School
Cary, North Carolina

Dan Barber
Teacher
Idlewild Elementary School
Charlotte, North Carolina

Brianne Beck
Teacher
Allen Jay Elementary School
High Point, North Carolina

Melissa Blush
Teacher
Allen Jay Elementary School
High Point, North Carolina

Ardelia Brown
Teacher
Pearsontown Elementary School
Durham, North Carolina

Alice M. Cook
Teacher
Paw Creek Elementary School
Charlotte, North Carolina

Lori D. Davis
Teacher
C. Wayne Collier Elementary School
Hope Mills, North Carolina

John D. Ellington
Former Director
Division of Social Studies
North Carolina Department of Public
   Instruction
Raleigh, North Carolina

Laura Griffin
Teacher
Sherwood Park Elementary School
Fayetteville, North Carolina

Sharon Hale
Teacher
Hillandale Elementary School
Durham, North Carolina

Dr. Ted Scott Henson
Educational Consultant
Burlington, North Carolina

Charlotte Heyliger
Teacher
C. Wayne Collier Elementary School
Hope Mills, North Carolina

Tony Iannone
Teacher
Nathaniel Alexander Elementary School
Charlotte, North Carolina

Judith McCray Jones
Educational Consultant
Former Elementary School
   Administrator
Greensboro, North Carolina

Gwendolyn C. Manning
Teacher
Gibsonville Elementary School
Gibsonville, North Carolina

Courtney McFaull
Teacher
Sherwood Park Elementary School
Fayetteville, North Carolina

Lydia Ogletree O'Rear
Teacher
Elmhurst Elementary School
Greenville, North Carolina

Marsha Rumley
Teacher
Brooks Global Studies
Greensboro, North Carolina

Dean P. Sauls
Teacher
Wayne County Public Schools
Goldsboro, North Carolina

Melissa Turnage
Teacher
Meadow Lane Elementary School
Goldsboro, North Carolina

Joseph E. Webb
Educational Consultant
Adjunct Professor
East Carolina University
Greenville, North Carolina

Harcourt
SCHOOL PUBLISHERS

Copyright © 2009 by Harcourt, Inc.

Printed in the United States of America

ISBN-13: 978-0-15-356637-0
ISBN-10: 0-15-356637-X

4 5 6 7 8 9 10 030 16 15 14 13 12 11 10

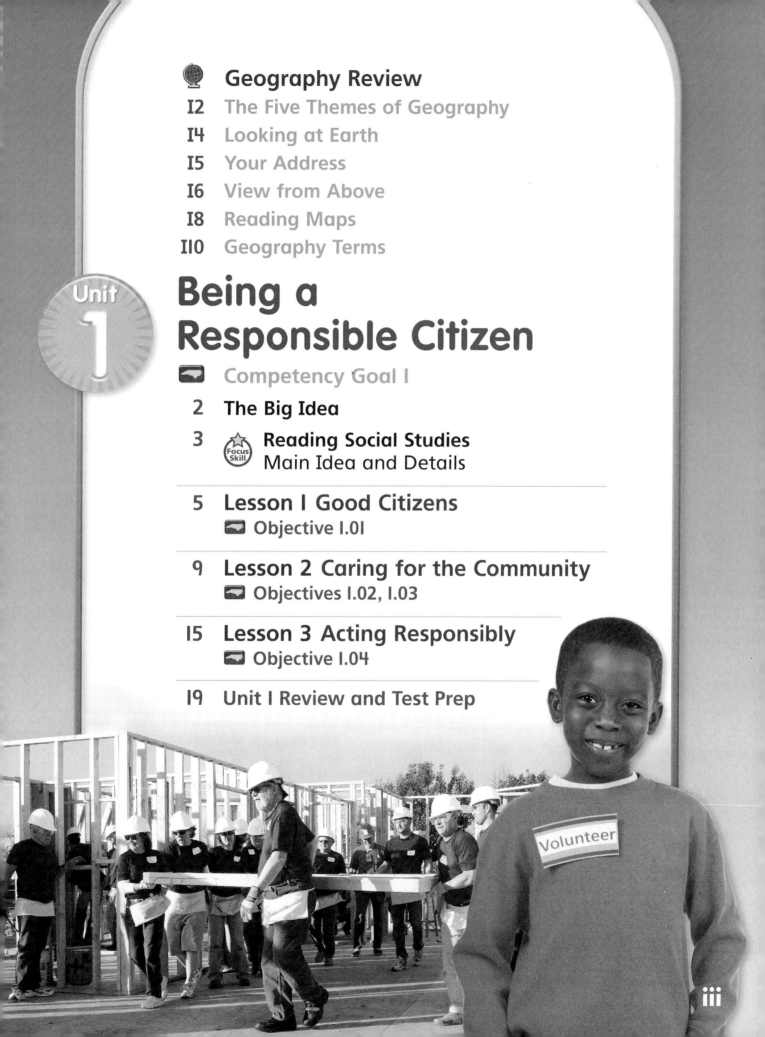

🌐 **Geography Review**

I2 The Five Themes of Geography

I4 Looking at Earth

I5 Your Address

I6 View from Above

I8 Reading Maps

I10 Geography Terms

Unit 1

Being a Responsible Citizen

Competency Goal 1

2 **The Big Idea**

3 (Focus Skill) **Reading Social Studies**
Main Idea and Details

5 **Lesson 1 Good Citizens**
Objective 1.01

9 **Lesson 2 Caring for the Community**
Objectives 1.02, 1.03

15 **Lesson 3 Acting Responsibly**
Objective 1.04

19 **Unit 1 Review and Test Prep**

Unit 2

People and Government

🔲 Competency Goal 2

24 **The Big Idea**

25 🌟 Focus Skill **Reading Social Studies**
Generalize

27 **Lesson 1 Taking Part**
🔲 Objective 2.05

31 **Lesson 2 Our Community Leaders**
🔲 Objective 2.01

37 **Lesson 3 Choosing Our Leaders**
🔲 Objective 2.02

41 **Lesson 4 Rules and Laws**
🔲 Objective 2.04

47 **Lesson 5 Citizens Work Together**
🔲 Objective 2.03

51 **Unit 2 Review and Test Prep**

A World of Many People

Competency Goal 3

56   **The Big Idea**

57   *(Focus Skill)* **Reading Social Studies**
       Recall and Retell

59   **Lesson 1 Our Different Roles**
       Objectives 3.01, 3.04

63   **Lesson 2 People and Cultures**
       Objectives 3.02, 3.03

71   **Lesson 3 Holidays and Celebrations**
       Objective 3.05

77   **Lesson 4 People Make a Difference**
       Objective 3.06

83   **Unit 3 Review and Test Prep**

Communities, Now and Long Ago

Competency Goal 4

88   **The Big Idea**

89   *(Focus Skill)* **Reading Social Studies**
       Sequence

91   **Lesson 1 Communities Change**
       Objective 4.01

95   **Lesson 2 Our Changing World**
       Objective 4.02

99   **Lesson 3 People Settle**
       Objective 4.03

103   **Unit 4 Review and Test Prep**

Unit 5

The World Around Us

Competency Goal 5

108 **The Big Idea**

109 **Reading Social Studies**
Focus Skill
Compare and Contrast

111 **Lesson 1 Geography Tools**
Objective 5.02

115 **Lesson 2 Finding Locations**
Objectives 5.04, 5.05

119 **Lesson 3 Our Land and Water**
Objective 5.01

125 **Lesson 4 Regions of North Carolina**
Objectives 5.03, 5.06

133 **Unit 5 Review and Test Prep**

Unit 6

Using Our Resources

Competency Goal 6

138 **The Big Idea**

139 (Focus Skill) **Reading Social Studies**
Cause and Effect

141 **Lesson 1 Using Our Natural Resources**
Objective 6.01

147 **Lesson 2 People Move**
Objective 6.03

151 **Lesson 3 Changing Our Physical Environment**
Objective 6.02

155 **Unit 6 Review and Test Prep**

Unit 7

People and the Marketplace

 Competency Goal 7

160 **The Big Idea**

161 **Reading Social Studies**
Categorize and Classify

163 **Lesson 1 Producers and Consumers**
Objectives 7.01, 7.02

169 **Lesson 2 Work and Income**
Objective 7.03

173 **Lesson 3 Spending Money**
Objective 7.04

177 **Lesson 4 Changing How We Use Resources**
Objective 7.05

181 **Unit 7 Review and Test Prep**

YOUR TAX DOLLARS AT WORK

Unit 8

Technology and Our World

 Competency Goal 8

186 **The Big Idea**

187  **Reading Social Studies**
Draw Conclusions

189 **Lesson 1 Using Technology**
Objectives 8.01, 8.02

195 **Lesson 2 Using Charts and Graphs**
Objective 8.03

201 **Unit 8 Review and Test Prep**

For Your Reference

R2 **Glossary**

R8 **Index**

Geography Review

I2   The Five Themes of Geography

I4   Looking at Earth

I5   Your Address

I6   View from Above

I8   Reading Maps

I10   Geography Terms

The Five Themes of Geography

The story of people is also the story of where they live. When scientists talk about Earth, they think about five themes, or main ideas.

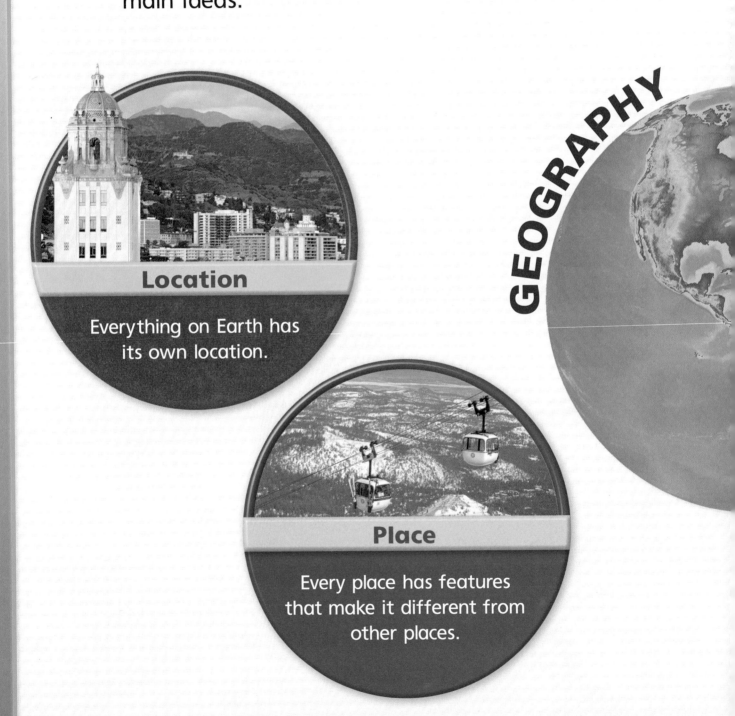

Location

Everything on Earth has its own location.

Place

Every place has features that make it different from other places.

GEOGRAPHY

Human-Environment Interactions

People can change the environment or find ways to fit into their surroundings.

Movement

People, goods, and ideas move every day.

THEMES

Regions

Areas of Earth share features that make them different from other areas.

Looking at Earth

The shape of Earth is shown best by a globe. A **globe** is a model of Earth.

On a map of the world, you can see all the land and water at once. A **map** is a flat drawing that shows where places are.

Much of the world is covered by large bodies of water called oceans.

A continent is one of seven main land areas on Earth.

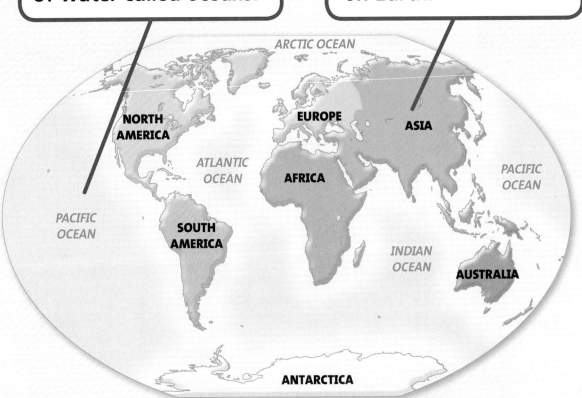

ARCTIC OCEAN

NORTH AMERICA

EUROPE

ASIA

ATLANTIC OCEAN

AFRICA

PACIFIC OCEAN

PACIFIC OCEAN

SOUTH AMERICA

INDIAN OCEAN

AUSTRALIA

ANTARCTICA

Name the seven continents and four oceans you see on the map.

Your Address

You live on the continent of North America in a country called the United States. Your address names the city and state in which you live.

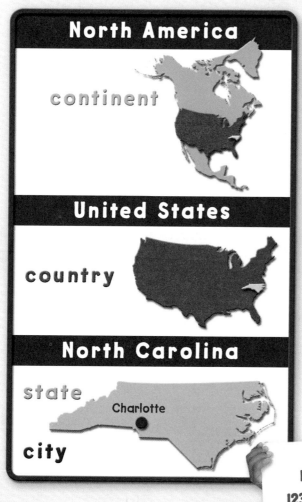

North America
continent

United States
country

North Carolina
state
Charlotte
city

Mari Tyler
123 Pine Street
Charlotte, NC 28269

What is your address?

View from Above

Does your neighborhood have a school, a grocery store, a library, a fire station, a park, and a bank? These are places that people share in a neighborhood. You can learn about a neighborhood by looking at a photograph.

How does a photograph taken from above help you study a neighborhood?

You can also learn about a neighborhood by looking at a map. Mapmakers draw symbols to help you find places on the map. A **map symbol** is a small picture or shape that stands for a real thing. The **map title** tells you what the map shows.

How is this map like the photograph? How is it different?

Neighborhood Map

Reading Maps

Maps are used to show many different kinds of information. This is a map of the United States. On this map, you can use the map key to find our national capital, or our country's capital. You can also use the key to find each state's capital and borders. A **border** is a line that shows where a state or country ends.

Locate the state of North Carolina on the map. What is the state capital? Name the states that border North Carolina.

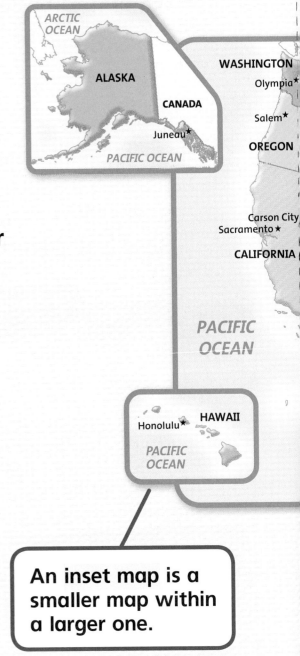

An inset map is a smaller map within a larger one.

Check the map title to see what area is being shown.

The United States

CANADA

MONTANA
★ Helena

NORTH DAKOTA
★ Bismarck

MINNESOTA

NEW HAMPSHIRE
VERMONT

MAINE
★ Augusta

Lake Superior

Montpelier ★

Concord
Boston

IDAHO
★ Boise

SOUTH DAKOTA
★ Pierre

St. Paul
★

WISCONSIN
Madison
★

MICHIGAN

Lake Huron

Lake Ontario

NEW YORK
Albany ★

MASSACHUSETTS
Providence

WYOMING

Lake Michigan

Lansing
★

Lake Erie

Hartford ★

RHODE ISLAND
CONNECTICUT

NEVADA

Cheyenne ★

IOWA
Des Moines
★

PENNSYLVANIA
Harrisburg ★

Trenton
NEW JERSEY

★ Salt Lake City

NEBRASKA
Lincoln ★

OHIO
Columbus
★

Dover
DELAWARE

UTAH

Denver ★

Topeka
★

Jefferson City ★

Springfield
★

Indianapolis
★

INDIANA

WEST VIRGINIA

Annapolis ★

Washington, D.C.

COLORADO

KANSAS

MISSOURI

Charleston
★

Frankfort
★

Richmond
★

MARYLAND

VIRGINIA

ARIZONA

Santa Fe ★

OKLAHOMA

KENTUCKY

Raleigh ★

NORTH CAROLINA

Phoenix ★

NEW MEXICO

Oklahoma City ★

ARKANSAS
Little Rock ★

TENNESSEE

Nashville ★

Columbia ★

SOUTH CAROLINA

ATLANTIC OCEAN

TEXAS

Austin ★

LOUISIANA

MISSISSIPPI

ALABAMA

GEORGIA

Atlanta ★

Jackson ★

Montgomery ★

Baton Rouge ★

Tallahassee ★

MEXICO

North
West ⊕ East
South

Gulf of Mexico

FLORIDA

Map Key
⊛ National capital
★ State capital
— Border

A compass rose shows directions. The cardinal directions are north, south, east, and west.

The map key shows what the symbols on the map mean. Symbols may be pictures, colors, patterns, lines, or other special marks.

Geography Terms

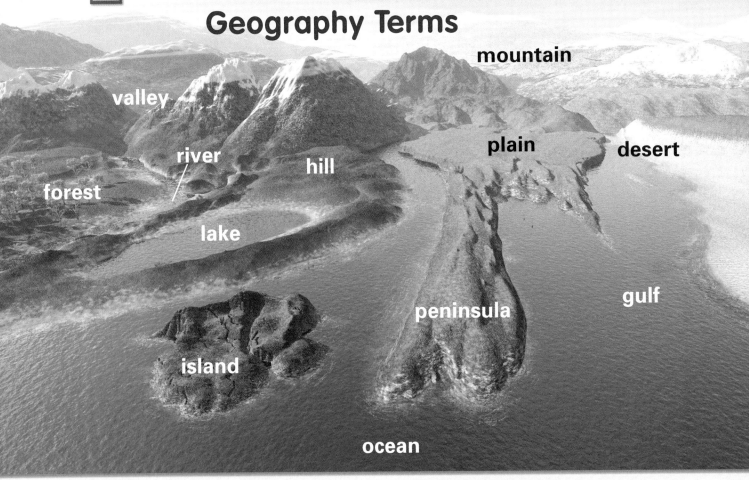

desert a large, dry area of land

forest a large area of land covered with trees

gulf a large body of ocean water that is partly surrounded by land

hill a landform that rises above the land around it

island land with water all around it

lake a body of water with land all around it

mountain the highest kind of landform

ocean a body of salt water that covers a large area

peninsula land that is surrounded on only three sides by water

plain flat land

river a large stream of water that flows across the land

valley low land between hills or mountains

Being a Responsible Citizen

Children raise a flag at Fort McHenry in Baltimore, Maryland.

Spotlight on Goals and Objectives

North Carolina Interactive Presentations

NORTH CAROLINA STANDARD COURSE OF STUDY

COMPETENCY GOAL 1 The learner will identify and exhibit qualities of responsible citizenship in the classroom, school, and other social environments.

 The Big Idea

How can citizens be responsible in their community?

Responsible citizens show respect for the people who live in their community. By following rules and helping others, responsible citizens make their community a good place to live.

Draw a picture that shows someone being responsible in your community.

Focus Skill Main Idea and Details

Learn

■ The main idea tells you what you are reading about. It is the most important idea.

■ The details explain the main idea.

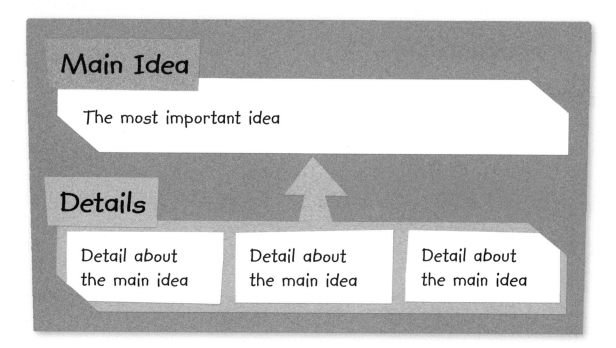

Main Idea

The most important idea

Details

| Detail about the main idea | Detail about the main idea | Detail about the main idea |

Practice

Underline one detail in the paragraph.

Volunteers are people who help others without being paid. Some volunteers build houses for people who need homes. Others clean up public places such as parks and beaches.

Main Idea

Detail

Apply

Read the following paragraph.

At Special Olympics events, children and adults with disabilities take part in sports. North Carolina hosts Special Olympics events at least twice a year. Volunteers help by raising money. They also help set up and clean up after Special Olympics events.

What details can you add to the chart below?

Main Idea

At Special Olympics events, children and adults with disabilities take part in sports.

Details

North Carolina hosts Special Olympics events at least twice a year.

_____
_____
_____

_____
_____
_____

Good Citizens

People who work and play together are part of a **community**. The people who live in and belong to a community are its **citizens.** Being a citizen comes with responsibilities. **What will you learn about being a citizen?**

_____

_____

Wilmington is a community in North Carolina.

NORTH CAROLINA
STANDARD COURSE OF STUDY

1.01 Identify and describe attributes of responsible citizenship.

❶ Underline four communities of which you are a part.

A Member of Many Communities

You are a part of many different groups called communities. You are a part of your family, your classroom, and your school. You also belong to a larger community. It is the city or town where you live. Citizens work together to make your city or town a good place to live, work, and play.

Our Responsibilities

Each citizen has a responsibility to make his or her community a good place to live. A **responsibility** is something that a person should take care of or do. Responsible citizens work together. They are also fair and honest.

At home, you can pick up your toys or set the table. You can be fair at school by sharing supplies. In the community, you can take turns when playing games.

TextWork

❷ Find the word responsibility. Underline the sentence that tells its meaning.

❸ Circle examples of children taking turns in the picture below.

7

1 **SUMMARIZE** How can a responsible citizen help make his or her community a good place to live?

_____

_____

_____

_____

2 Write a sentence using the words **citizen** and **responsibility**.

_____

_____

3 Why is it important to treat others fairly?

_____

_____

Writing

What are some of your responsibilities in your family, at school, and in your community?

Caring for the Community

People have responsibilities at home, at school, and in the community. They are responsible for taking care of the community. Caring for the community helps everyone. **What will you learn about taking responsibility?**

_____

_____

**NORTH CAROLINA
STANDARD COURSE OF STUDY**

1.02 Demonstrate responsible citizenship in the school, community, and other social environments.

1.03 Analyze and evaluate the effects of responsible citizenship in the school, community, and other social environments.

1 Underline examples of family responsibilities in the text.

2 Circle examples of children acting responsibly in the picture below.

Acting Responsibly

You have responsibilities as a member of your family. You are responsible for keeping your room clean. You might do other chores, too. You might clean up after meals or take out the trash.

At school, children also have responsibilities. They need to listen in class. Children must finish their schoolwork on time. Members of clubs and sports teams must work together and play fairly.

Helping Others

People who are responsible care about others. They help take care of the community. Some people called **volunteers** work without being paid. A volunteer spends some of his or her free time helping other people. People who volunteer help make the community a better place to live.

TextWork

3 Who spends free time helping other people?

_____

Volunteers care for others in many ways.

North Carolina Volunteers

Hurricane Katrina damaged communities in Mississippi, Louisiana, and Alabama in 2005. The town of Bay St. Louis, Mississippi, was destroyed. The community of Southern Pines, North Carolina, wanted to help.

The people in Southern Pines raised more than $80,000 for the people of Bay St. Louis. Volunteers from Southern Pines went to Bay St. Louis to rebuild homes, schools, and other buildings.

TextWork

4 Which North Carolina community sent volunteers to Bay St. Louis, Mississippi?

_____

_____

Volunteers help people build homes across the United States.

Aubyn and Welland are from Hickory, North Carolina. When Aubyn was ten years old and Welland was seven years old, they started a group called Suitcases for Kids.

This group collects suitcases for foster children when they move. Foster children are children who live with other families. Today, volunteers across the United States collect suitcases.

TextWork

5 Who received the suitcases from Aubyn and Welland's group?

_____

_____

Lesson 2 Review

1 **SUMMARIZE** How is helping others a way to take care of the community?

_____

_____

_____

2 List two examples of things that **volunteers** can do.

_____

_____

_____

3 Why do people volunteer?

_____

_____

_____

Activity

Make a poster that shows one way people help others in your community.

Acting Responsibly

Jennifer has just moved to New Bern, North Carolina. She wants to be a responsible citizen. She knows that there are consequences to her actions. A **consequence** is what happens because of what a person does. **What will you learn about acting responsibly?**

_____

_____

NORTH CAROLINA STANDARD COURSE OF STUDY

1.04 Identify responsible courses of action in given situations and assess the consequences of irresponsible behavior.

Consequences

Jennifer is responsible and respectful. There are consequences for her actions. She helps her family set and clear the dinner table. Because she helps, the job is done faster. Jennifer raises her hand to answer questions in class. Because Jennifer raises her hand, her teacher calls on her. Jennifer looks both ways before crossing the street. By waiting, she stays safe from traffic.

What if Jennifer did not help set and clear the table? It would take longer to get the job done. In class, Jennifer knows that children who do not raise their hands may not be called on.

Jennifer also knows that if she crosses the street without looking both ways, she could be hurt. Knowing the consequences of her actions helps Jennifer be responsible and respectful.

TextWork

3 Underline the sentences that describe the consequences of not acting responsibly.

1 **SUMMARIZE** What are the consequences of being responsible in your community?

_____

_____

_____

2 What is a **consequence** of not being responsible?

_____

_____

3 Why do you think it is important for all members of a community to act responsibly?

_____

_____

Writing

Think of something you are responsible for doing at school. What is the consequence of doing or not doing your task?

Review and Test Prep

 The Big Idea

Citizens can be responsible in their communities.

Summarize the Unit

Focus Skill **Main Idea and Details** Fill in the graphic organizer with ways to be a responsible citizen.

Main Idea

Responsible citizens help make the community a good place to live, work, and play.

Details

They work together and are fair and honest.

_____

_____

_____

_____

_____

_____

_____

_____

Use Vocabulary

Complete each sentence.

Word Bank

community
  p. 5
citizen
  p. 5
responsibility
  p. 7
volunteer
  p. 11
consequence
  p. 15

1 A _____ is something that

a person should take care of or do.

2 People who work and play together are

part of a _____.

3 A _____ is what happens

because of what a person does.

4 A person who lives in and belongs to a

community is its _____.

5 A _____ spends time helping

others without being paid.

20

Think About It

Circle the letter of the correct answer.

6 To be called on in class, you should

    A pick up your toys

    B set and clear the dinner table

    C look both ways before crossing the street

    D raise your hand

7 Which is a way to show responsibility at home?

    A listening in class

    B working together in clubs

    C keeping your room clean

    D finishing schoolwork on time

8 Who are the people who help with Suitcases for Kids?

    A volunteers

    B members of clubs

    C citizens

    D members of a sports team

9 Which is the largest community to which people belong?

    A their family

    B their city or town

    C their classroom

    D their school

Answer each question in a complete sentence.

10 What do you think would happen if there were no consequences for the ways people act?

_____

_____

11 What are some ways people can treat others fairly at school and in the community?

_____

_____

Show What You Know

Writing Write a Diary Entry
Describe one group you are in. Tell who else is part of that group. What do you think is important about the group?

Activity Design a Volunteer Poster
What kind of volunteer group could you start to help others? Make a poster for your new volunteer group.

GO online To play a game that reviews the unit, join Eco in the North Carolina Adventures online or on CD.

People and Government

City Hall and Courthouse, Asheville, North Carolina

Spotlight on Goals and Objectives

North Carolina Interactive Presentations

NORTH CAROLINA STANDARD COURSE OF STUDY

COMPETENCY GOAL 2 The learner will evaluate relationships between people and their governments.

 # The Big Idea

How do the people of a community take part in government?

The people who live in a community take part in government. They make choices about their leaders and about how to act in their community. The government works for the people in the community. It helps people be safe and get along with one another.

Draw a picture of a government leader in your community.

Generalize

Learn

■ To generalize is to make a statement about a group of facts.

■ To generalize, think about how the facts are related.

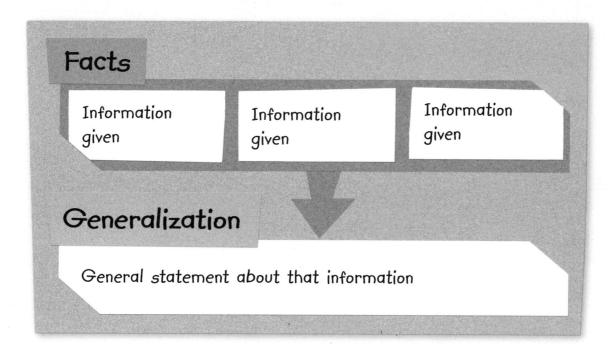

Facts

| Information given | Information given | Information given |

Generalization

General statement about that information

Practice

Underline the generalization in the paragraph below.

The Constitution of the United States is a set of laws. It protects Americans' freedoms. The Constitution makes the United States the free and fair country it is today.

Fact

Apply

Read the following paragraph.

The Constitution of the United States was signed on September 17, 1787. In 2006, President George W. Bush signed a law making Constitution Day a national holiday. On September 17, people get together to read the first part of the Constitution. They also learn about the 39 people who signed it.

What facts can you add to the chart below?

Facts

In 2006, President George W. Bush signed a law making Constitution Day a national holiday.

_____
_____
_____
_____

_____
_____
_____
_____

Generalization

Constitution Day helps people learn about the Constitution.

Responsible citizens **participate**, or take part, in their social environments. **Social environments** are places in which people meet to work or play in the community. What will you learn about ways citizens take part in their communities?

_____

_____

NORTH CAROLINA STANDARD COURSE OF STUDY

2.05 Identify examples of responsible citizen participation in society and social environments.

School Activities

You have a choice in how you take part in social environments. You might belong to a sports team. You might work with others on an art activity.

In any social environment, you have a responsibility to do your share. Members of a group must work together. They must respect each other. A group is only as good as its members make it.

TextWork

1 Name two examples of social environments.

Sports team
art group

2 Circle a sentence that tells how members of groups should work.

Community Activities

Some social environments in a community are parks and playgrounds. You have a responsibility to take care of places that you share with others.

If you see litter at the park, what could you do? You could make a sign asking people not to litter. You could also help by cleaning up the litter.

 **TextWork**

3 Circle the picture that shows someone taking care of a social environment.

1 **SUMMARIZE** What are some responsible ways in which people can participate in their communities?

_____

_____

_____

2 What is a **social environment**?

_____

_____

3 Why is it important for people to participate in their communities?

_____

_____

_____

Writing

Make a list of the social environments in which you participate.

Our Community Leaders

A leader is a person who helps others get a job done. Some leaders are part of the **government**, or group of citizens that runs a community. Government leaders work to keep people safe and to keep order. **What do you think you will learn about community leaders?**

_____

_____

New County Courthouse in Durham, North Carolina

NORTH CAROLINA STANDARD COURSE OF STUDY

2.01 Identify and explain the functions of local governmental bodies and elected officials.

1 Circle in the text the three kinds of community leaders.

2 What is a judge in <u>charge</u> of?

_____

Community Government

Most community governments have three kinds of leaders. The **mayor** is the leader of a town or a city. The **council** is a group that makes decisions for the community. Courts are another part of community government. **Judges** are in charge of the courts.

Judges decide whether someone has broken a law. A **law** is a rule that people in a community must follow. A **rule** tells people what must or must not be done.

Government Leaders		
Mayor	Council	Judge
• Leads a city or town • Makes sure community laws are followed	• Makes decisions for the community • Works with the mayor	• In charge of a court • Decides whether someone has broken a law

Mayor

Terry Bellamy is the mayor of Asheville, North Carolina. Her job is to make sure the community is a good place to live. Mayors make sure that things like roads, schools, and parks are well kept.

As mayor, Terry Bellamy works with the members of Asheville's city council. Together they make decisions for the community.

Mayor

Mayor Terry Bellamy of Asheville

Council Member

Donna Shannon is a member of the town council in Aberdeen, North Carolina. The council meets to talk about and solve any problems in the community.

Many councils decide how much money to collect from citizens. Then they decide how to spend the money. They decide where to build places for people to live and work. The council works with the mayor to make laws.

TextWork

4 Circle in the text Donna Shannon's job in the government.

5 Who works with a council to make laws?

Town Council

Donna Shannon of Aberdeen town council

34

Judge

Courts are another part of community governments. People may go to court if someone has broken the law or to solve problems.

Orlando Hudson, Jr., works as a judge in the courts of Durham County, North Carolina. Judge Hudson decides whether people have broken the law. He also decides what the consequences will be for people who have broken the law.

 **TextWork**

6 Underline the sentence that describes why people might go to court.

Judge

The Honorable Orlando Hudson, Jr., of Durham County

Lesson 2 Review

1 **SUMMARIZE** How do local leaders work for the people of a community?

_____

_____

_____

2 How are **rules** and **laws** related?

_____

_____

3 Why is it important for mayors and council members to work together?

_____

_____

_____

Writing

Write a letter to your community's council members about a law you think your community needs.

Choosing Our Leaders

Citizens in the United States choose most of their government leaders at events called **elections**. They choose leaders they think will do the best job for each level of government. The three levels are local, state, and national. **What will you learn about choosing leaders?**

_____

_____

Before elections, people explain why citizens should vote for them.

NORTH CAROLINA
STANDARD COURSE OF STUDY

2.02 Recognize and demonstrate examples of the elective process.

Elections

Each community decides when to hold elections for local leaders. Local leaders are people such as mayors and city council members. Some state leaders are elected every four years. The governor of North Carolina is a state leader. The President of the United States is elected every four years, too. The President is a national leader. The national government is the government of the whole country.

TextWork

1 How often is the President of the United States elected?

_____

_____

2 Circle three kinds of leaders named in the text.

North Carolina
state seal

North Carolina's governor Mike Easley is sworn into office.

Voting

Before citizens vote, they decide who will do the best job. A **vote** is a choice that is counted. Citizens vote by marking a ballot. A **ballot** is a list of all the choices. Voters mark their choices in secret.

After everyone has voted, the ballots are counted. The winner of an election is the person who gets the most votes. Voting is a fair way for groups to make choices.

TextWork

3 Circle the person in the picture below who is voting.

4 Underline the sentence that tells who the winner of an election is.

Citizens take part by voting.

39

1 **SUMMARIZE** Explain how government leaders are chosen.

_____

_____

_____

2 How do citizens use a **ballot** in an **election**?

_____

_____

3 Why do you think people vote in secret?

_____

_____

_____

Activity

Imagine that your class is electing a class president. Make a poster asking people to vote for you.

Rules and Laws

All groups have rules and laws that must be followed. The government makes laws to protect people's rights. If people break laws, they may have to work for the community or pay money. **What will you learn about rules and laws?**

_____

_____

NORTH CAROLINA STANDARD COURSE OF STUDY

2.04 Evaluate rules and laws and suggest appropriate consequences for noncompliance.

Rules

![TextWork]

1 Underline rules children must follow at home and at school.

2 Circle the sign below that shows the consequence for littering.

People must follow the rules of their groups. At home, children must put away toys. At school, children must put away school supplies. People must wait their turn in lines.

If a child breaks a rule at school, the consequence might be to miss playtime. If a person does not wait his or her turn in line, the consequence may be to go to the end.

Laws

Everyone must follow laws. Traffic laws help keep people safe. Without traffic laws, people might get into many accidents. Police make sure the government's laws are followed.

People who break laws must face the consequences. They may have to pay money or do work for the community. People who break certain laws are put in jail.

TextWork

3 Underline the sentences that explain why people must follow traffic laws.

Street signs show laws everyone must follow.

4 Where are the rights and freedoms of Americans explained?

_____

_____

5 Circle the picture of someone using freedom of speech.

Rights and Freedoms

There are laws against not respecting the rights and freedoms of others. A **right** is a kind of freedom that people have. Having **freedom** means being able to make your own choices. When people respect one another's rights, everyone's rights are protected.

Biography

Fairness

Ella Josephine Baker

Ella Josephine Baker grew up in Littleton, North Carolina. She has always cared deeply about fairness. As an adult, she worked to make sure that all people had the same rights. In 1952, she became the leader for the National Association for the Advancement of Colored People, which works for equal rights for African Americans.

Our rights and freedoms are explained in the Constitution of the United States. The **Constitution** is a written set of laws. Our government must protect the rights listed in the Constitution.

One right is freedom of speech. Other rights are freedom of the press, freedom of religion, and the right to meet peacefully in groups.

Freedom of the Press

Freedom of Religion

The Constitution

Freedom of Speech

1 **SUMMARIZE** Why are rules and laws important in a community?

_____

_____

_____

2 What is one of your **rights** as a citizen?

_____

_____

3 Why must people face consequences for breaking rules and laws?

_____

_____

_____

Activity

Think of a rule in your classroom or at your school. Draw a picture that shows people following the rule.

Citizens Work Together

People, families, and communities depend on one another. Citizens help to make their community a good place to live. The government provides services called **government services** for the citizens. **What will you learn about how people depend on one another?**

_____

_____

MORRISON REGIONAL LIBRARY

Public library in Charlotte, North Carolina

NORTH CAROLINA
STANDARD COURSE OF STUDY

2.03 Describe the interdependence among individuals, families, and the community.

Government Services

Everyone who lives in a community uses government services. In an emergency, you can call 911. Fire and police departments will come to help. These government services help keep citizens safe.

Delivering mail, taking care of parks, and collecting garbage are government services. Buses and subways are also government services.

Community governments can provide services because the citizens pay taxes. A **tax** is money paid to the government. The government uses taxes to pay for services. Taxes pay for things in communities, such as schools, parks, and libraries. Tax money is also used to fix streets and to buy police cars and fire engines. Government services help make communities safe and good places to live.

TextWork

❸ Who pays taxes?

_____

❹ Underline some ways taxes are used.

Firefighters help keep communities safe.

Lesson 5 Review

1 **SUMMARIZE** How do people and their communities depend on one another?

_____

_____

_____

2 Why does a government collect **taxes**?

_____

_____

3 What might happen if citizens did not pay taxes?

_____

_____

_____

Writing

Write a thank-you note to someone in the government for providing a service. Tell how the service has helped you.

Review and Test Prep

 The Big Idea

People of a community take part in government.

Summarize the Unit

Focus Skill Generalize Fill in the chart to show how people should work together in a group.

Facts

Members of a group have a responsibility to do their share.

_____

_____

_____

_____

_____

_____

Generalization

A group is only as good as its members make it.

Use Vocabulary

Fill in the blanks with the correct words.

Word Bank

participates
p. 27
government
p. 31
law
p. 32
Constitution
p. 45
taxes
p. 49

Mrs. Arnold takes part, or

1 _____, in our community.

She participates by following every

2 _____. The

3 _____ is a written set of

laws for the government to follow. Mrs.

Arnold also participates by voting, or

helping choose the people who run our

community. This group of citizens, called a

4 _____, helps everyone get along.

Mrs. Arnold helps the government do its work

by paying **5** _____ to the

government.

52

Think About It

Circle the letter of the correct answer.

6 What is the leader of a state called?

    A mayor

    B governor

    C judge

    D council member

7 Which of these lists the rights of all citizens?

    A Constitution

    B government

    C ballot

    D President

8 Who decides whether someone has broken a law?

    A a mayor

    B a governor

    C a judge

    D a council member

9 What are roads, schools, parks, and libraries?

    A taxes

    B courts

    C ballots

    D government services

Answer each question in a complete sentence.

10 How do laws help keep citizens safe?

_____

_____

11 Why is it important to vote in elections?

_____

_____

Show What You Know

Writing Write a Letter
Think about something that would help the citizens of your community stay safe. Write a letter to the mayor telling how your idea would help.

Activity Role Play
Role-play how a city council makes new laws. Practice presenting your ideas. Use costumes and props. Role-play a council meeting and write a new law.

GO online To play a game that reviews the unit, join Eco in the North Carolina Adventures online or on CD.

A World of Many People

Square dance convention in Louisville, Kentucky

Spotlight on Goals and Objectives

North Carolina Interactive Presentations

NORTH CAROLINA STANDARD COURSE OF STUDY

COMPETENCY GOAL 3 The learner will analyze how individuals, families, and communities are alike and different.

The Big Idea

How are people, families, and communities alike and different?

The world is made up of many people. Every person belongs to different groups, such as their family and their community. Families may have different ways of life. Communities can be large or small.

Draw a picture of you and a friend. Show how you are alike. Show how you are different.

Reading Social Studies

Recall and Retell

Learn

■ To recall is to remember.

■ To retell is to tell about something in your own words.

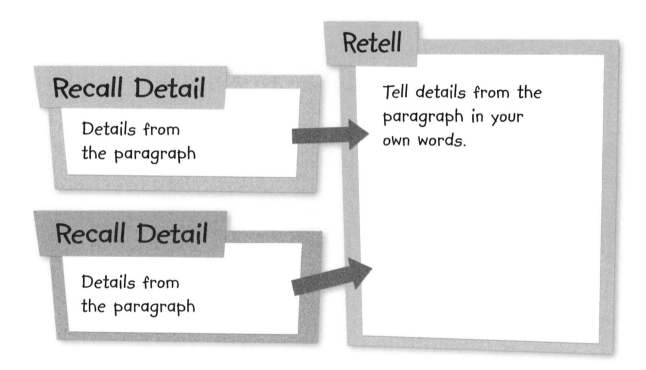

Retell

Tell details from the paragraph in your own words.

Recall Detail

Details from the paragraph

Recall Detail

Details from the paragraph

Practice

Underline two details that you can use to retell the paragraph.

Long ago, many people from Scotland came to live in North Carolina. Today, almost as many Scottish people live in the United States as live in Scotland.

Detail

Apply

Read the following paragraph.

Every July, the Grandfather Mountain Highland Games are held in Linville, North Carolina. These games celebrate the culture of people from Scotland. You can see traditional Scottish clothing. You can watch Scottish games and dancing and eat Scottish foods. You can also learn about the history of the Scottish people.

What can you add to the chart below?

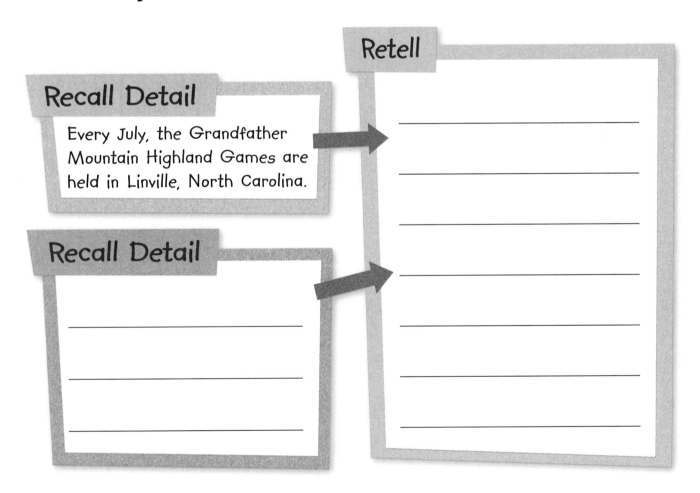

Retell

Recall Detail

Every July, the Grandfather Mountain Highland Games are held in Linville, North Carolina.

Recall Detail

Our Different Roles

A community is made up of many people. One way we are alike and different is in the roles we play. A **role** is the part a person plays in a group or community. **What might you learn about different roles?**

_____

_____

Being a team member is one role that children can have.

NORTH CAROLINA STANDARD COURSE OF STUDY

3.01 Compare similarities and differences between oneself and others.

3.04 Identify multiple roles performed by individuals in their families and communities.

How We Are Different

People are both alike and different in the ways they look, act, think, and feel. In some ways you are like your friends, classmates, and other people around the world. In some ways, you are different.

People like to do different things. They like different books and sports. Some like to live in big cities. Others like to live in small towns.

TextWork

❶ In the first paragraph, underline four ways people can be alike and different.

❷ Do different and alike have the same or opposite meanings?

Biography

Respect

Amy Tan

Amy Tan was born in Oakland, California, in 1952. When she was young, Amy Tan used her imagination to write. Today, she writes stories about her family. Amy Tan is an American who remembers the Chinese traditions of her family's past. She uses her writing to honor her family's history.

How We Are Alike

People belong to the same kinds of groups. In each group, they have their own roles. At home, children may be brothers or sisters, and adults may be parents. At school, children are students, and adults are teachers.

In the community, adults may be many kinds of workers, such as police officers and firefighters. Some adults work as mail carriers or doctors.

TextWork

❸ What is the role that children have at school?

_____

❹ In the text, circle the roles of community workers.

1 **SUMMARIZE** How do people's roles make them both like and different from others?

_____

_____

_____

2 What is a **role**?

_____

_____

3 How will your roles be different when you are older?

_____

_____

_____

Writing

Make a list of roles you have in your family, at school, and in your community.

People and Cultures

Lesson 2

People show their **culture**, or ways of life, in different ways. They eat different foods, wear different clothes, and speak different languages. **Language** is the words or signs we use to communicate. What might you learn about culture?

_____

_____

Sharing our cultures helps us learn from and understand one another.

**NORTH CAROLINA
STANDARD COURSE OF STUDY**

3.02 Describe similarities and differences among families in different communities.

3.03 Compare similarities and differences among cultures in various communities.

A Family from Mexico

María's family has lived in Arizona for a long time. The adults have passed on their Mexican heritage to their children. **Heritage** is the culture that is passed down from family to family.

María likes to play old Mexican songs on her guitar. These songs are part of her family's heritage. María's Spanish-style home reminds her of her family's heritage.

TextWork

❶ Underline two examples of María's family heritage.

❷ Circle the same examples in the pictures below.

Mexico

64

A Family from Korea

Kim's grandmother helps him and his family members learn about their Korean culture. She shows Kim pictures of the family's ancestors, who lived in South Korea. **Ancestors** are family members who lived long ago.

Kim's grandparents moved from South Korea to the United States as immigrants. An **immigrant** is a person who comes from another place to live in a country.

TextWork

❸ Underline how Kim's grandmother teaches the family about Korean culture.

❹ What do we call family members who lived long ago?

_____

South Korea

65

A Family from Russia

Ben's great-grandfather moved his family from Russia to New York in 1927. Ben's family is Jewish. They live in a neighborhood with other families from Russia. Ben's family enjoys watching Russian dancers. Ben has a <u>matryoshka</u>, or set of Russian nesting dolls.

The family works together. They also go to synagogue together to follow their religion. **Religion** is a set of beliefs about God or gods.

TextWork

5 Where is Ben's great-grandfather from?

_____

6 Underline the sentence that tells what the word <u>religion</u> means.

Russia

A Family from Pakistan

Aneesa and her family moved to the United States from Pakistan. Pakistan is a country in Asia. They are learning English and making friends in their new country.

Aneesa's family follows the religion of Islam. Sometimes they wear traditional clothes. A **tradition** is something that is passed on from older family members to children.

 TextWork

7 Where is Pakistan?

_____

8 Circle the picture that shows Aneesa and her family wearing traditional clothing.

Pakistan

A Family in Ghana

Abena lives in Ghana, a country in Africa. The people in her village sell fruits, vegetables, and crafts at the market. They speak English and a language called Twi.

The children listen to folktales told in Twi. A **folktale** is a story passed on over time. Many of the stories are about Anansi the spider. The people of Ghana say that it was Anansi who brought stories to the world.

TextWork

9 Circle the picture that shows people getting vegetables ready to sell at the market.

10 What languages does Abena speak?

_____

_____

Ghana

ANANSI a tale from the Ashanti **THE SPIDER** by Gerald McDermott

Henry Holt

A Family in Spain

Eduardo lives with his family in Cordoba, a city in Spain. He and his family follow Spanish customs. A **custom** is a way of doing something.

Eating together is a custom that is part of family life in Spain. Lunch is the biggest meal of the day. Many businesses close at lunchtime so that people can go home to eat with their families.

TextWork

⑪ Underline the sentence that tells what a custom is.

⑫ Circle a custom shown in the pictures below.

Spain

1 **SUMMARIZE** How are families and cultures alike
and different in communities around the world?

_____

_____

_____

2 Write a sentence using the word **folktale**.

_____

_____

3 Why do you think some people move to a
new country?

_____

_____

_____

Writing

What customs and traditions has your
family passed on over time?

Holidays and Celebrations

Holidays are days on which people celebrate or remember culture, events, and heroes. **Heroes** are people who have done something brave or important. **What will you learn about holidays and celebrations?**

_____

_____

At the Aloha Festivals in Hawaii, people celebrate their Hawaiian culture.

**NORTH CAROLINA
STANDARD COURSE OF STUDY**

3.05 Identify historical figures and events associated with various cultural traditions and holidays celebrated around the world.

Celebrating Heroes

In the United States, we celebrate Dr. Martin Luther King, Jr., Day in January. Dr. King worked to change unfair laws. In February, we celebrate Presidents' Day. On Memorial Day in May, we honor those who gave their lives for our country in wars. In the Philippines, people celebrate National Heroes Day in August. They remember people who have done good things for their country.

❶ Underline four holidays that honor heroes.

❷ Circle the celebration of Memorial Day in the pictures below.

Memorial Day

George Washington, first President of the United States

Dr. Martin Luther King, Jr.

72

Celebrating Independence

In the United States, people also celebrate events, such as getting their independence. **Independence** is the freedom of people to choose their own government.

We celebrate Independence Day on the Fourth of July. Juneteenth is on June 19. It celebrates the end of slavery for African Americans. In France, people celebrate Bastille Day on July 14. That was the start of their fight for independence.

✏️ TextWork

3 Which holiday celebrates the end of slavery?

_____

Juneteenth

Bastille Day

Independence Day

④ In the text, circle the holidays on which people celebrate their traditions.

⑤ Circle the holiday celebrated by Mexican Americans in the pictures below.

Celebrating Traditions

People celebrate their traditions with music, food, and special clothing. Japanese people celebrate Hanami, when the cherry blossom trees bloom. They go on picnics and enjoy the trees. On May 5, Mexicans and Mexican Americans celebrate Cinco de Mayo. People dress up, play music, and dance. African Americans celebrate Kwanzaa in December. They remember African traditions.

Cinco de Mayo

Kwanzaa

74

Celebrating the New Year

People all around the world celebrate the New Year. Chinese people celebrate their New Year with parades and gifts. In India, people celebrate Diwali, or the Festival of Lights. They gather with family members and decorate their homes.

At Rosh Hashanah, Jewish people eat special foods and go to synagogue. At Maal Hijra, Muslims think about the past year and go to mosques.

 TextWork

6 What is the name for the Jewish New Year?

_____

7 Circle the Festival of Lights in the pictures below.

Diwali

Chinese New Year

75

1 **SUMMARIZE** What kinds of holidays and cultural traditions do people around the world celebrate?

_____

_____

_____

2 Why do we remember **heroes** with holidays?

_____

_____

3 Why do you think people celebrate holidays?

_____

_____

_____

Activity

Choose a person that you would like to honor with a holiday. Draw a picture that shows how this holiday would be celebrated.

People Make a Difference

Lesson 4

People have different ideas and talents. By sharing them, they can make a difference in their communities. We can learn from our **diversity**, or different ideas and ways of living. **What will you learn about making a difference?**

_____

_____

The Nobel Prize is awarded to people who help others.

NORTH CAROLINA STANDARD COURSE OF STUDY

3.06 Identify individuals of diverse cultures and describe their contributions to society.

Working for Fairness

Citizens in a community can do their part to work for fairness.

TextWork

1 Underline how Jackie Robinson helped others.

2 Circle the reason Sojourner Truth changed her name.

Jackie Robinson

Jackie Robinson grew up being treated differently because of the color of his skin. He worked hard, went to college, and served in the Army. He was the first African American to play major league baseball. He helped other African Americans to be treated fairly.

Sojourner Truth

Sojourner Truth was first named Isabella Van Wagener. A sojourn is a journey. She changed her name because she wanted to travel and tell the truth. Sojourner Truth spoke against slavery because she believed it was wrong.

Caring for Others

By caring for others, people can make their communities better places to live.

TextWork

3 Circle the reason Mother Teresa won the Nobel Peace Prize.

4 What did Clara Barton start?

_____

_____

_____

Mother Teresa

Mother Teresa spent her life caring for people around the world. She provided food, clothing, and shelter for the people who needed help. She won the Nobel Peace Prize for her good works.

Clara Barton

Clara Barton worked all her life to help people. She cared for hurt soldiers during the American Civil War. She also started the American branch of the Red Cross. The Red Cross helps people when bad things happen, such as floods.

Serving Others

Many people take part in their communities as leaders who serve the people.

Golda Meir

Golda Meir was a Russian immigrant to the United States. Later, she moved to Israel. She believed that the Jewish people should have their own homeland. At the age of 71, she became Israel's first woman leader.

Elizabeth Duncan Koontz

Education was important to Elizabeth Duncan Koontz. She became a teacher. Later, she worked with many teachers' organizations in North Carolina. She was the first African American president of the National Education Association.

Helping Others

People can use their talents, ideas, and hard work to help their communities.

 **TextWork**

7 Underline the way Dr. Greer helped people in Miami.

8 Circle the groups in which Elaine Chao has been a leader.

Dr. Pedro José Greer, Jr.

Dr. Pedro José Greer, Jr., started a clinic to help people in Miami. He has also written a book, given advice to Presidents, and received many awards. Today he continues to help those in need.

Elaine Chao

Elaine Chao moved from Taiwan to the United States when she was eight years old. She became the leader of the Peace Corps and the United Way. She was the first Asian American to work in the President's Cabinet. Her job was Secretary of Labor.

1 **SUMMARIZE** What are some ways people can make a difference in their communities?

_____

_____

_____

2 How do the people in this lesson show **diversity**?

_____

_____

3 Why are people who make a difference in their community often called heroes?

_____

_____

_____

Writing

How can you make a difference in your community?

Review and Test Prep

 The Big Idea

People, families, and communities are alike and different.

Summarize the Unit

Focus Skill **Recall and Retell** Fill in the chart to show what you have learned about holidays which celebrate independence.

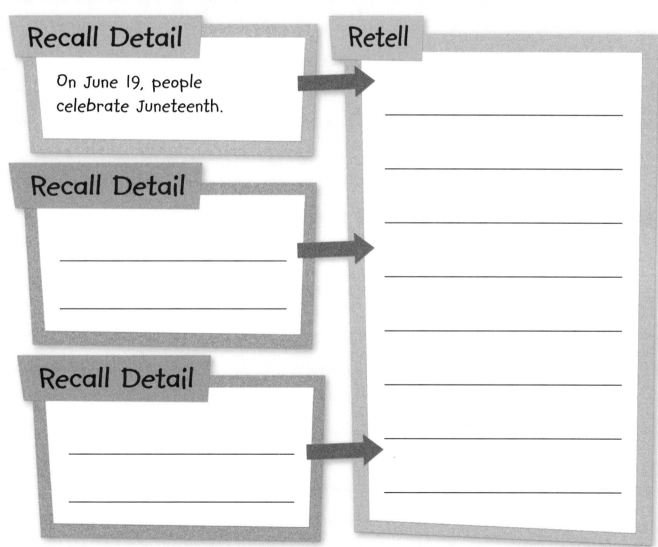

Recall Detail

On June 19, people celebrate Juneteenth.

Recall Detail

_____

_____

Recall Detail

_____

_____

Retell

_____
_____
_____
_____
_____
_____
_____
_____
_____
_____

Use Vocabulary

Complete each sentence.

Word Bank

role
  p. 59
culture
  p. 63
immigrants
  p. 65
custom
  p. 69
diversity
  p. 77

❶ Kim's grandparents were

_____ when they moved

from South Korea to the United States.

❷ It is a _____ for Eduardo and

his family to eat lunch together each day.

❸ A _____ is the part a person

plays in a group or community.

❹ We can learn from our _____, or

different ideas and ways of living.

❺ Language, clothing, and food are ways people

can express their _____, or ways

of life.

84

Think About It

Circle the letter of the correct answer.

6 Which is a family role?

    A doctor

    B parent

    C student

    D police officer

7 On which holiday do we remember heroes?

    A Rosh Hashanah

    B Kwanzaa

    C Memorial Day

    D Juneteenth

8 Who traveled and spoke out against slavery?

    A Sojourner Truth

    B Dr. Pedro Jose Greer, Jr.

    C Elizabeth Duncan Koontz

    D Elaine Chao

9 What are the words and signs we use to communicate?

    A tradition

    B ancestor

    C heritage

    D language

Answer each question in a complete sentence.

⑩ What are some ways people can be alike and different?

_____

_____

⑪ List some countries and groups that celebrate their independence.

_____

_____

Show What You Know

Writing Write a Diary Entry
Think about a holiday your family celebrates. Write a diary entry about the day or days you celebrate this holiday.

Activity Design a Storyboard
Design a family history storyboard. Interview family members. Collect photographs or draw pictures of events. Put the pictures in order.

GO online To play a game that reviews the unit, join Eco in the North Carolina Adventures online or on CD.

Communities, Now and Long Ago

Downtown
Greensboro,
North Carolina

**Spotlight on Goals
and Objectives**

North Carolina Interactive Presentations

**NORTH CAROLINA
STANDARD COURSE OF STUDY**

COMPETENCY GOAL 4 The learner will
exhibit an understanding of change in
communities over time.

The Big Idea

How do people and places change over time?

People and places change over time. To change is to become different. As communities change, people must decide where to live and how to use the land around them. The ways people look, think, and feel can change, too.

Draw a picture of something that has changed in your life or in your community.

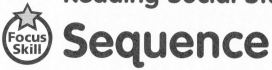 Sequence

Learn

■ Sequence is the order in which events happen. What happens first? What happens next? What happens last?

■ As you read, look for sequence words, such as <u>first</u>, <u>next</u>, <u>then</u>, <u>later</u>, <u>finally</u>, and <u>last</u>. These words give sequence clues.

First	Next	Last
What happens first	What happens next	What happens last

Practice

Read the paragraph below. Underline the sentence that tells what happened after New Bern became the state capital.

First, people began moving to North Carolina in the 1500s. Next, New Bern became the state capital. Last, the capital of North Carolina was changed to Raleigh.

Sequence

Apply

Read the following paragraph.

Andrew's grandfather moved to North Carolina when he was 20 years old. First, he built a small house. Next, he found a job on a farm. He harvested vegetables and helped with the cattle. Last, he used the money he saved to buy his own farm. Today, Andrew lives in the house that his grandfather built long ago.

The chart below shows the sequence of events in Andrew's grandfather's life. What can you add to the chart?

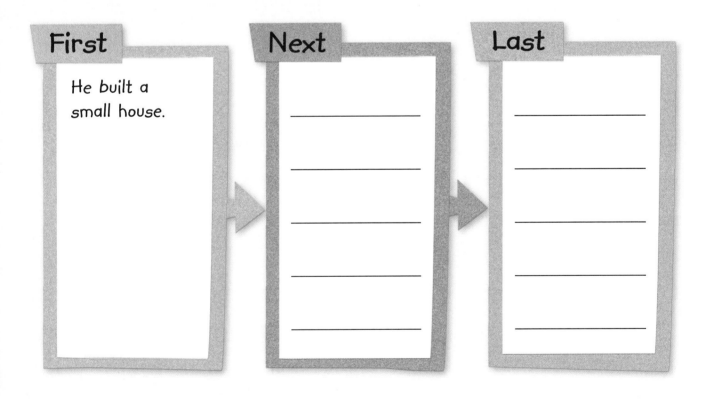

First	Next	Last
He built a small house.	_____	_____

Communities Change

People and places **change**, or become different, over time. History tells about people and places and how they have changed. **History** is the study of things that took place in the past. **What will you learn about change?**

_____

_____

New buildings change a community near Raleigh, North Carolina.

NORTH CAROLINA STANDARD COURSE OF STUDY

4.01 Analyze the effects of change in communities and predict future changes.

① Underline the sentence that describes what present means.

② Which comes first, the present or the future?

_____

A Family Changes

Katie lives in Marietta, Ohio. Her grandparents tell her about what their lives were like in the past. The **past** is the time before now. Katie thinks about what her family is like in the present. The **present** is the time right now.

Katie also thinks about her life in the **future**, or the time yet to come. When Katie is older, she may go to college and have a job.

Changes in the Community

Like many places, Marietta looked different long ago. The community was smaller then. Over time, more people have moved into the community.

Today, people are building new houses and new roads. If Marietta keeps growing, the community may build new schools and parks.

 TextWork

❸ Underline ways Marietta has changed over time.

❹ Circle the picture that shows how Marietta looks today.

1 **SUMMARIZE** How can communities change over time?

_____

_____

_____

2 How is the **past** different from the **future**?

_____

_____

3 How do you think your community may change in the future?

_____

_____

_____

Writing

✎ Look at some pictures from the past. Write about how the things they show are different from the things you see today.

Our Changing World

Our **environment** is all the things around us. Plants, animals, and people are part of the environment. Changes in the environment can affect the way people live. **What will you learn about changes to the environment?**

_____

_____

Asheville, North Carolina

NORTH CAROLINA STANDARD COURSE OF STUDY

4.02 Analyze environmental issues, past and present, and determine their impact on different cultures.

1 Underline the text that explains what happened to the American Indians after the environment changed.

2 What makes the air, water, or land dirty?

_____

3 Circle the picture that shows people helping animals.

The Environment Long Ago

Over time, the environment has changed. Long ago, American Indians used the land for growing and gathering food. They also used animals, such as buffalo.

New settlers also hunted buffalo. Soon few buffalo were left. People built cities on land that used to be forests. The environment had changed. The ways of life of the American Indians had to change, too. They could no longer use the land as they once did.

The Environment Today

One problem the environment faces today is pollution. **Pollution** is anything that makes the air, water, or land dirty. If we do not have clean water and air, then people, plants, and animals will be hurt. For example, when the ocean becomes polluted, fishers cannot catch as many fish for food. To help, people can clean up the oceans.

People take part in a sea turtle rescue program in Topsail Beach, North Carolina.

There are rules that keep the Outer Banks of North Carolina clean and healthy for plants and animals.

Lesson 2 Review

1 **SUMMARIZE** How did changes to the environment change the way that people lived?

_____

_____

_____

_____

2 What is the **environment**?

_____

_____

3 Why is it important for people to try not to pollute the environment?

_____

_____

_____

Activity

Make a poster showing how people in your community have changed the environment.

Most communities long ago were small. Communities grew as more people moved into them. Some communities became large cities. Some people moved to quieter areas near the cities. Others still lived in the country. **What will you learn about where people settled?**

_____

_____

A neighborhood in Charlotte, North Carolina

**NORTH CAROLINA
STANDARD COURSE OF STUDY**

4.03 Describe human movement in the establishment of settlement patterns such as rural, urban, and suburban.

Rural Areas

Kendra's family lives on a farm in Waynesville, a rural area of North Carolina. **Rural** areas are often in the countryside, far from a city. Rural areas can be quiet places to live.

People in rural areas can use the land there to grow food and raise animals. They use wood from the trees for building homes. Many people also sell things from rural areas to people in other places.

TextWork

❶ Circle the ways people in rural areas can use land.

❷ What is a suburb near?

_____

❸ On the map, what color shows where the most people live?

_____

Rural

Urban

Urban and Suburban Areas

Michael's family lives in Asheville, a city in North Carolina. A city is an **urban** area. It has many homes, apartments, and businesses. A city is full of people and things to do.

John's family lives in Grace, a suburb near Asheville. A **suburb** is a smaller community near a city. Suburbs have less traffic and quieter neighborhoods. Some people live in a suburb and work in the city.

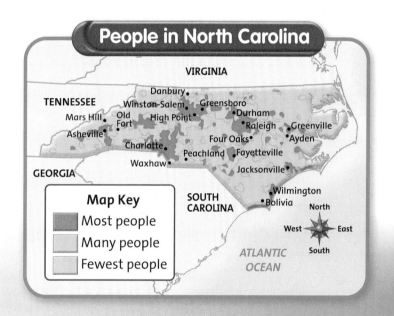

People in North Carolina

VIRGINIA

TENNESSEE

Danbury

Winston-Salem   Greensboro
Mars Hill   Old   High Point   Durham
    Fort   Raleigh   Greenville
Asheville   Four Oaks   Ayden
    Charlotte
    Peachland   Fayetteville
    Waxhaw   Jacksonville

GEORGIA

SOUTH
CAROLINA   Wilmington
    Bolivia

ATLANTIC
OCEAN

North
West   East
South

Map Key
- Most people
- Many people
- Fewest people

Suburb

1 **SUMMARIZE** What are some of the reasons people choose to live in a place?

_____

_____

_____

2 How is a **suburb** different from a **rural** area?

_____

_____

3 What could cause a city to be a busy place?

_____

_____

_____

Writing

Is your community a rural, an urban, or a suburban community? Give examples to support your answer.

Review and Test Prep

 The Big Idea

People and places change over time.

Summarize the Unit

(Focus Skill) **Sequence** Fill in the chart to show how the community of Marietta, Ohio, has changed over time.

First

The community was smaller.

Next

_____

_____

_____

_____

_____

_____

_____

Last

_____

_____

_____

_____

_____

_____

_____

103

Use Vocabulary

Write the word under its meaning.

❶ plants, animals, and people are

part of it

_____

❷ anything that makes the air, water, or

land dirty

_____

❸ what happens when something becomes

different

_____

❹ a kind of area that has many homes,

apartments, and businesses

_____

❺ the time that is yet to come

_____

Think About It

Circle the letter of the correct answer.

6 What is an area in the countryside called?

    A rural

    B urban

    C suburb

    D environment

7 What is the time that comes before the present called?

    A change

    B the time yet to come

    C the past

    D the time right now

8 What is the time right now called?

    A the past

    B history

    C the future

    D the present

9 What can people do to help if oceans are polluted?

    A study history

    B clean up the oceans

    C use the land for growing food

    D build new houses and roads

Answer each question in a complete sentence.

10 Why do you think some people live in suburbs?

_____

_____

11 What does history tell us about?

_____

_____

Show What You Know

Writing Write About You
Think of events from your life you would like to share. Write a paragraph about events from your past and in the present. Put the events in sequence.

Activity Do Research
Use the library or the Internet to find out about problems with the environment today. Make a list of what people are doing to help solve the problems.

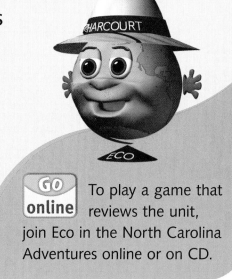

GO online To play a game that reviews the unit, join Eco in the North Carolina Adventures online or on CD.

The World Around Us

Skiers on
Sugar Mountain,
Avery County,
North Carolina

Spotlight on Goals and Objectives

North Carolina Interactive Presentations

**NORTH CAROLINA
STANDARD COURSE OF STUDY**

COMPETENCY GOAL 5 The learner will
understand the relationship between
people and geography in various
communities.

 # The Big Idea

How can geography help people learn about the places around them?

Geography helps people learn about the way places look. Geography can help people understand weather and climate. Geography tools, such as maps and globes, can show the kinds of land and water found on Earth. Geography tools also help people find places.

Draw a picture that shows the geography of your community.

Compare and Contrast

Learn

■ To compare, think about how people, places, or things are alike.

■ To contrast, think about how they are different.

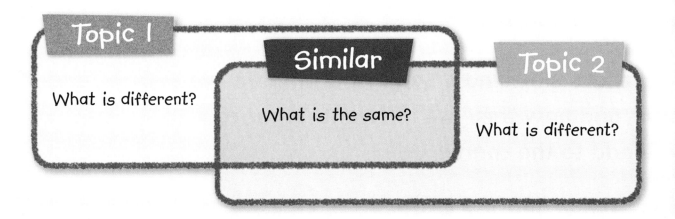

Topic 1

What is different?

Similar

What is the same?

Topic 2

What is different?

Practice

Read the paragraph below. Underline the sentence that tells how the Rocky River and the Chowan River are the same.

The Rocky River and the Chowan River are both rivers in North Carolina. The Rocky River flows into the Pee Dee River. The Chowan River flows into Albemarle Sound.

Topic 1

Topic 2

Apply

Read the following paragraph.

Sylva and Manteo are two cities in North Carolina. Visitors to Sylva can shop on Main Street, hike in the mountains, and see waterfalls. Visitors to Manteo can fish in the ocean, see a lighthouse, and visit a boat museum. In both cities, people can enjoy a number of activities.

This chart shows how Sylva and Manteo are alike and how they are different. What can you add to the chart?

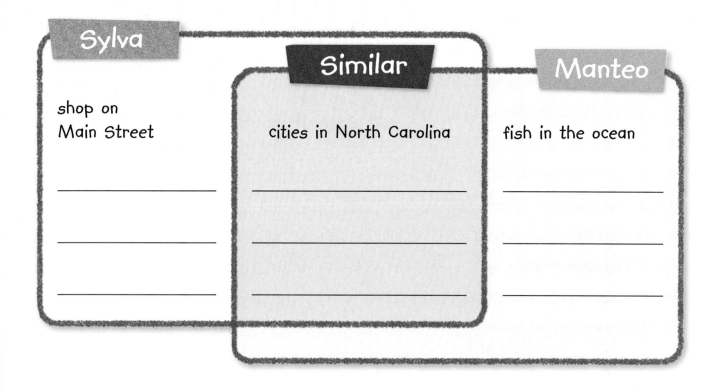

Sylva

shop on
Main Street

_____

_____

_____

Similar

cities in North Carolina

_____

_____

_____

Manteo

fish in the ocean

_____

_____

_____

Geography Tools

Geography is the study of Earth and its people. A **geographer** is a person who studies geography. Geographers use tools such as maps, globes, compasses, and photographs. Geographers use these tools to describe places. **What will you learn about geography tools?**

_____

_____

A farm near Cruso, North Carolina

NORTH CAROLINA STANDARD COURSE OF STUDY

5.02 Describe the role of a geographer and apply geographic tools, such as maps, globes, compasses, and photographs, in the understanding of locations and characteristics of places and regions.

111

Maps

![TextWork icon] **TextWork**

❶ On the map, circle the state in which you live.

❷ On the map, mark an X through the states that are around your state.

There are many kinds of maps. Some maps show small areas, such as parks or neighborhoods. Other maps show large areas, such as cities, states, and countries.

A map does not always show the true shapes on Earth. This is because maps are flat and Earth is round. A map also does not show the true sizes of the oceans and continents. However, a map can show all the land and water at once.

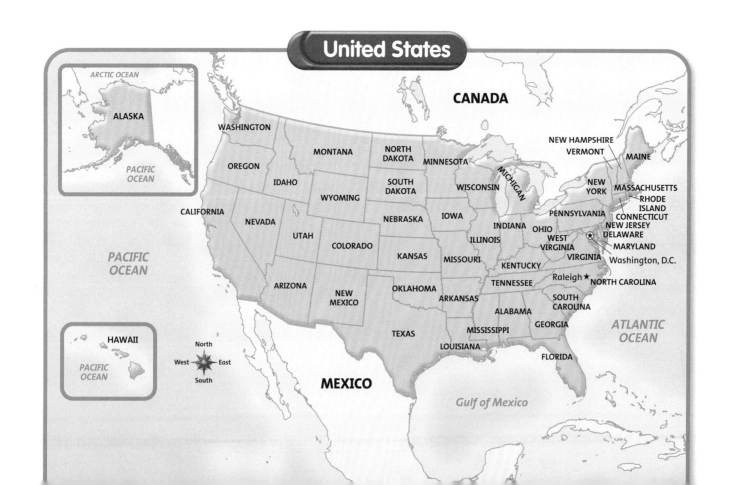

United States

Globes

The round shape of Earth is shown best by a globe. Because of its shape, a globe can only show one-half of Earth at a time.

People can use a compass to find directions. Cardinal directions are north, south, east, and west. South is the direction of the South Pole. North is toward the North Pole. When you face north, east is to your right and west is to your left.

 **TextWork**

3 What shape are both Earth and a globe?

_____

4 In the text, underline the four cardinal directions.

Compass

Globe

Cardinal directions

113

1. **SUMMARIZE** How can using geography tools help you learn about Earth and the places on it?

_____

_____

_____

2. How are the words **geography** and **geographer** related?

_____

_____

3. Compare and contrast maps and globes. How are they alike? How are they different?

_____

_____

_____

Writing

Write a paragraph that tells where North Carolina is in the United States. Use cardinal directions in your paragraph.

Finding Locations

By reading a map, a person can see how to get from one place to another. Charts and pictures can also help people find locations. **What will you learn about finding locations?**

_____

_____

Blue Ridge Parkway, North Carolina

**NORTH CAROLINA
STANDARD COURSE OF STUDY**

5.04 Identify the absolute and relative location of communities.
5.05 Interpret maps, charts, and pictures of locations.

TextWork

1 What does relative location help you find on a map?

_____

_____

2 Circle the words with the same meaning as <u>absolute location</u>.

Relative Location and Absolute Location

You can use maps to find what a place is near, or the **relative location**. For example, look at the map of the World's Fair Park. You can see that the candy factory is near the art museum.

You can also use maps to find the **absolute location**, or exact location, of a place. For example, a street address is an absolute location.

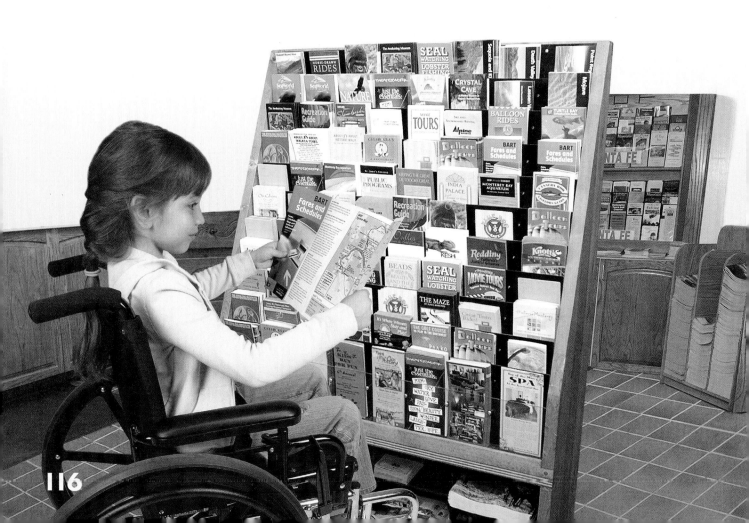

Using Maps and Charts

Look at the map grid below. A **map grid** is a set of lines that divides a map into columns and rows of squares.

Put your finger on the picture of the art museum. Slide your finger left. This is row B. Put your finger on the art museum again. Slide your finger up. This is column 4. The art museum is at B-4.

 **TextWork**

3 In the map grid below, what is in square C-1?

_____

4 Locate square D-5 on the map grid below. Add a picture of a pet store to D-5.

World's Fair Park

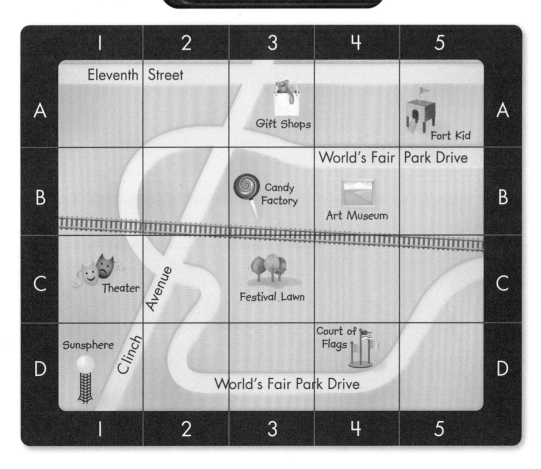

① **SUMMARIZE** How do maps, charts, and pictures help people find locations?

_____

_____

_____

② How can a **map grid** help people understand a map?

_____

_____

③ How is the relative location of your school different from its absolute location?

_____

_____

_____

Activity

Make a map of your community. Trace how to get from your house to your school.

Our Land and Water

There are many different landforms and bodies of water on Earth. A **landform** is a kind of land with a special shape. The weather and climate of places also tell us about Earth. **What might you learn about land and water?**

_____

_____

Whitewater Falls, North Carolina

NORTH CAROLINA STANDARD COURSE OF STUDY

5.01 Define geography and use geographic terms to describe landforms, bodies of water, weather, and climate.

Landforms

North America is not the same everywhere. If an eagle flew across North America, it would see many different landforms and bodies of water.

In the middle of our country, the eagle would see plains. Plains are flat land. The eagle would also see land with many hills. A hill is land that rises above the land around it. A **mountain** is a very high hill. A group of mountains is called a mountain range.

Hills

Mountains

The eagle might fly over land that has water around it on all sides but one. This land is a **peninsula**. An **island** is a landform with water all around it. The Outer Banks are islands along the coast of North Carolina. The **coast** is the part of the land that touches the ocean.

✎ **TextWork**

❸ How many sides of a peninsula are NOT surrounded by water?

_____

❹ Circle the picture of the island.

Island

Coast

Great Smoky Mountains
National Park, North Carolina

Bodies of Water

TextWork

5 Underline the sentence that describes a gulf.

6 Circle the names of lakes and rivers in North Carolina.

The biggest bodies of water are oceans. Oceans cover most of Earth. Sometimes, land partly surrounds a large body of water. This body of water is a gulf.

All over the land, there are rivers and lakes. A river is a stream of water that flows across the land. The Cape Fear River is in North Carolina. A lake is a body of water that has land all around it. Fontana Lake is in North Carolina.

Gulf

River

Weather and Climate

Weather is the way the outside air feels. One day the weather might feel sunny and warm. Many people visit the beaches of North Carolina. Another day it might be cloudy and cool. It can snow in the mountains of North Carolina. Many people ski in the snow.

Climate is the kind of weather a place has over a long time. Many mountain regions have a cool climate. Coastal regions usually have a warm climate.

TextWork

7 In what kind of weather would you want to play at the beach?

_____

_____

8 Underline the sentence that describes <u>climate</u>.

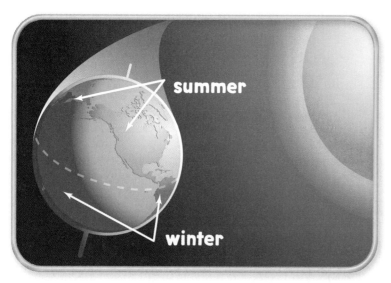

On Earth, it is summer in places tilted towards the sun. It is winter in places tilted away from the sun.

1 **SUMMARIZE** What kinds of landforms and bodies of water make up Earth?

_____

_____

_____

_____

2 What is a **landform**? List examples of some landforms.

_____

_____

3 Where is it summer on Earth? Where is it winter?

_____

_____

Activity

Draw a map of North America. Label its countries, major bodies of water, and major landforms, such as mountains, hills, and plains.

Different parts of the country are grouped into regions. A **region** is an area of land with the same features. North Carolina has three regions. Each region has different **physical features**, or land, water, climate, and plant life. **What will you learn about regions?**

_____

_____

Cape Hatteras Lighthouse, Buxton, North Carolina

NORTH CAROLINA STANDARD COURSE OF STUDY

5.03 Compare and contrast the physical features of communities and regions.

5.06 Identify and describe the people, vegetation, and animal life specific to certain regions and describe their interdependence.

The Mountain Region

The western part of North Carolina is called the Mountain region. The Blue Ridge and the Great Smoky mountains both run through this region. Mount Mitchell is in this region, too. It is the highest point east of the Mississippi River.

Several rivers flow through the Mountain region. One is the Little Tennessee River, and another is the French Broad River.

 **TextWork**

1 What is the highest point east of the Mississippi River?

_____

2 Underline the names of mountains found in the Mountain region.

3 Circle the pictures that show people using the physical features of the Mountain region.

Mountain Region

VA

TN

NORTH CAROLINA

GA   SC   ATLANTIC OCEAN

Trees cover most mountains in this region. People of the Mountain region use wood from the trees to build homes and furniture. The forests are home to many animals, such as bears and deer.

Many people visit the region to see its mountains and animals. Winters can be very cold. It snows a lot. Many people enjoy hiking in the Mountain region.

Making furniture

Hiking

Mount Mitchell is in the Black Mountains of North Carolina.

Piedmont Region

VA

TN

NORTH CAROLINA

GA SC ATLANTIC OCEAN

The Piedmont Region

The center of North Carolina is called the Piedmont region. Piedmont means "foot of the mountain." Rolling hills cover this part of North Carolina. Much of the ground is clay. Potters use the clay to make dishes to sell.

There are many large lakes and rivers in the Piedmont region. Lake Norman and High Rock Lake are in the Piedmont region. The Deep River and the Haw River are also in this region.

Trees grow in the western half of the Piedmont region. Small mammals and birds live in this region. The weather is usually mild and sunny. People can farm and raise animals in the hilly land of the Piedmont.

Most people in North Carolina live in the Piedmont. The biggest cities in North Carolina are in this region. Raleigh, the capital of North Carolina, is there. Charlotte, Greensboro, Winston-Salem, and Durham are in the Piedmont, too.

 **TextWork**

6 In which region do most people in North Carolina live?

_____

_____

Many people work in downtown Charlotte, North Carolina.

7 In which part of North Carolina is the Coastal Plain region?

_____

8 Underline the words that describe a cape.

Coastal Plain Region

VA

TN

NORTH CAROLINA

GA   SC   ATLANTIC OCEAN

The Coastal Plain Region

The Coastal Plain region is in the eastern part of North Carolina. It borders the Atlantic Ocean. In this region, the land is flat. Along the coast are many bays and capes. A **bay** is a smaller body of water that is partly surrounded by land. A **cape** is a point of land that sticks out into water. There are also miles of islands called the Outer Banks.

A farm in Hyde County, North Carolina

The Coastal Plain has wetlands, or swampy areas. The wetlands are home to many kinds of plants and animals. Alligators, sea turtles, and many kinds of birds live in the Coastal Plain.

A white ibis in the Outer Banks, North Carolina

Much of the Coastal Plain is used for farming. The soil is very good for growing crops. People in the Coastal Plain region grow cotton, peanuts, wheat, and soybeans. Fishers work in this region. People enjoy the many beaches along the North Carolina coast.

Lesson 4 Review

1 **SUMMARIZE** How are the three regions of North Carolina alike? How are they different?

_____

_____

_____

2 What are some **physical features** of North Carolina?

_____

_____

3 How are the people, land, and animals of each region in North Carolina related?

_____

_____

_____

Writing

Write a paragraph that describes the physical features, plants, animals, and ways people live in your region.

132

Review and Test Prep

 The Big Idea

Geography helps people learn about the land, water, and places around them.

Summarize the Unit

Compare and Contrast Fill in the chart to show how features of two regions in North Carolina are alike and different.

Piedmont

hills

_____

_____

_____

_____

_____

_____

Similar

trees

_____

_____

_____

_____

_____

_____

Coastal Plain

borders ocean

_____

_____

_____

_____

_____

_____

Use Vocabulary

Write the word under its meaning.

1 an area of land with the same features

_____

2 a person who studies geography

_____

3 a kind of land with a special shape

_____

4 the exact location of a place

_____

5 the study of Earth and its people

_____

Word Bank

geography
  p. 111
geographer
  p. 111
absolute
location
  p. 116
landform
  p. 119
region
  p. 125

Think About It

Circle the letter of the correct answer.

6 Which is a tool used by a geographer?

    A a compass rose

    B a region

    C a cape

    D a climate

7 Which best describes a mountain?

    A flat land

    B a peninsula

    C a body of water

    D a very high hill

8 How are different parts of the country grouped?

    A as oceans

    B as cardinal directions

    C as regions

    D as mountain ranges

9 What is the kind of weather a place has over a long time?

    A climate

    B a cape

    C a region

    D an island

Answer each question in a complete sentence.

10 How does relative location help you understand where a place is?

_____

_____

11 Why might maps not show the true shapes of places on Earth?

_____

_____

Show What You Know

Writing Write a Letter
Write a letter to a pen pal about a place in or near your community. Include a map that shows the place you tell about.

Activity Make an Atlas
Research one region of Earth using the library or the Internet. Make a page that shows the plants, animals, landforms, and climate of the region.

GO online To play a game that reviews the unit, join Eco in the North Carolina Adventures online or on CD.

Using Our Resources

A cotton field in the Tennessee Valley in Alabama

Spotlight on Goals and Objectives

North Carolina Interactive Presentations

NORTH CAROLINA STANDARD COURSE OF STUDY

COMPETENCY GOAL 6 The learner will analyze how people depend on the physical environment and use natural resources to meet basic needs.

 # The Big Idea

How do people use natural resources to meet their needs?

The environment includes natural resources, such as trees, air, water, and soil. People use natural resources in many ways. They might use trees to build homes. Water and air can be used to make electricity.

Draw a picture of a natural resource that you use.

Cause and Effect

Learn

■ A cause is an event or action that makes something happen.

■ An effect is the thing that happens because of a cause.

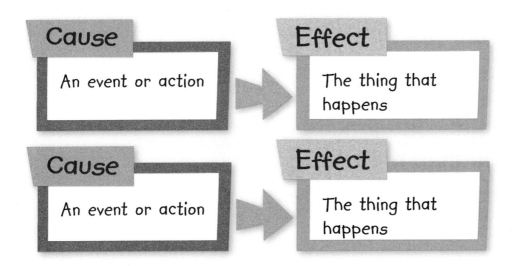

Practice

Read the paragraph below. Underline the the effect of Ernesto watering the seeds.

Ernesto wanted to grow his own bean plant in a cup with soil. At first, he forgot to water the seeds, so they did not grow. When he watered the seeds, they began to grow.

Cause

Effect

Apply

Read the following paragraph.

The ways people in North Carolina use the land depend on the region in which they live. In the Coastal Plain region, people are near the ocean. As a result, they raise and catch fish to sell. In the Piedmont region, much of the soil is clay. People make the clay into bricks to sell. In the Mountain region, many trees grow. People use the trees to build homes and furniture.

This chart shows the ways people in North Carolina use the land in the regions where they live. What can you add to the chart?

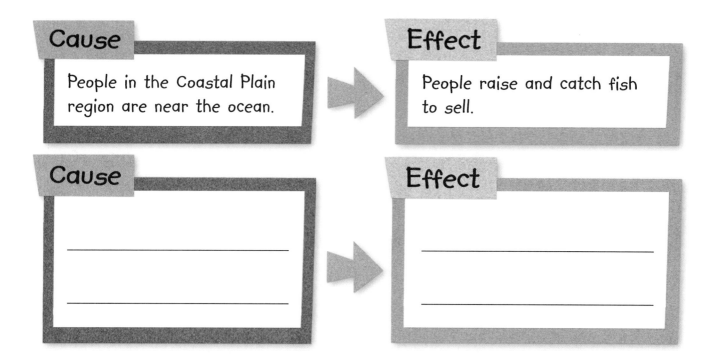

Cause

People in the Coastal Plain region are near the ocean.

Effect

People raise and catch fish to sell.

Cause

_____

_____

Effect

_____

_____

Using Our Natural Resources

People use natural resources to meet their needs. A **natural resource** is something found in nature, such as water, air, trees, and soil. People must use these resources responsibly. **What will you learn about natural resources?**

_____

_____

Farmers use soil to grow plants.

**NORTH CAROLINA
STANDARD COURSE OF STUDY**

6.01 Identify natural resources and cite ways people conserve and replenish natural resources.

141

Using Water

All living things need water to live. People use water for drinking, cooking, and bathing. They also use it for washing clothes and cleaning. People use water to grow plants, too. People also use water to go places in boats or ships.

Water can also be used to make electricity. People build dams on rivers. Inside a dam, the flow of the river turns big machines. The machines make electricity.

TextWork

❶ Circle three ways people use water.

❷ Underline the sentences that describe how a dam works.

❸ Circle the pictures that show how people use natural resources.

Wolf Creek Dam in Kentucky

Using Air and Trees

People, plants, and animals also need clean air to live. Like water, air can be used to make electricity. Wind turbines use the wind's energy to make electricity.

People use trees in many ways. Some trees grow fruits and nuts that people use for food. Wood from trees can be used to build homes and furniture. Wood can also be used to make paper.

Trees are a very useful natural resource.

Wind Turbines

Using Soil and Fuel

TextWork

4️⃣ Circle the examples of crops grown in North Carolina.

5️⃣ Underline the sentence that describes fuel.

People use soil to grow crops. A **crop** is a plant people grow for food or for other needs. People in North Carolina grow many crops, such as sweet potatoes, cotton, tomatoes, and soybeans.

People can find other natural resources under the ground. Coal, oil, and natural gas are found underground. People dig and drill for these resources and make them into fuels. A **fuel** is something that can be burned for heat or energy.

Protecting Resources

We all must help protect Earth's resources. **Conservation** is the saving of resources to make them last longer. To conserve water and electricity, turn off water and lights when they are not being used.

Recycling is another way to save resources. To **recycle** is to use the materials in old things to make new things. Some resources can be replaced. When people cut down trees, they can plant new ones.

Most paper, plastic, and aluminum can be recycled (below). Recycling food garbage can keep soil healthy (right).

TextWork

6 Underline the sentence that describes the effect conservation has on resources.

7 Circle the pictures that show people recycling resources.

145

Lesson 1 Review

1 **SUMMARIZE** What natural resources do people use? How can we protect these resources?

_____

_____

_____

2 What do we do when we **recycle**?

_____

_____

3 What might happen if people do not protect natural resources?

_____

_____

_____

Writing

Make a list of the natural resources you use in one day. Describe how you can conserve or replace these resources.

People Move

The physical environment can affect where people live and how they travel. People may change the physical environment to make travel easier. How people travel has changed over time. **What might you learn about how people move?**

_____

_____

People can travel by horse-drawn carriage in Colonial Williamsburg, Virginia.

**NORTH CAROLINA
STANDARD COURSE OF STUDY**

6.03 Identify means and methods of human movement as they relate to the physical environment.

① Since traveling by boat was once the fastest way to travel, where did many people live?

_____

Transportation Long Ago

Transportation is the moving of things and people from place to place. Long ago, transportation was slow. Boats were the fastest way to travel. As a result, many people lived near water.

Later, people built train tracks across the United States. Trains and streetcars helped move people and things more quickly.

Transportation Changes

It was not easy to cross some landforms. It was hard for people to travel over mountains. To make travel easier, people made trails through mountain passes. Later, they built roads.

After the automobile was invented, people could travel faster and farther. Today, airplanes help people cross land and water quickly.

TextWork

2 What landforms were hard for people to cross?

_____

3 Underline the sentence that tells the effect of the invention of the automobile.

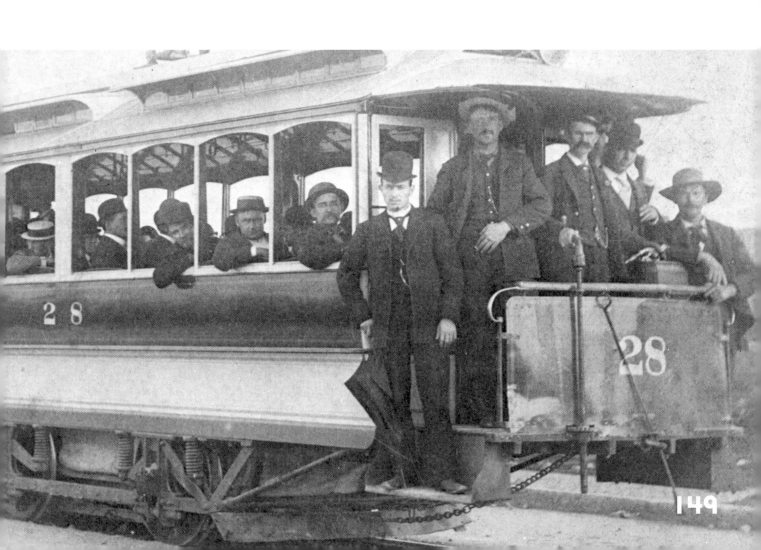

1 SUMMARIZE How does the physical environment affect how people move?

_____

_____

_____

2 What is **transportation**?

_____

_____

3 How has transportation changed over time?

_____

_____

_____

Activity

Make a poster showing different kinds of physical environments. Show the kind of transportation that would be used in each.

Changing Our Physical Environment

Lesson

3

People **modify**, or change, the physical environment to meet their needs. When people modify the land, there are consequences. **What will you learn about how people modify the environment?**

_____

_____

People change the land to build homes in California.

**NORTH CAROLINA
STANDARD COURSE OF STUDY**

6.02 Cite ways people modify the physical environment to meet their needs and explain the consequences.

151

Modifying the Land

Sometimes people must modify the land before they can build communities or grow crops. They may have to cut down trees, move rocks, or make tunnels through mountains. People may drain lakes to make more land to build on. By changing the physical environment, people are able to live in many different places.

TextWork

❶ Underline examples of how people modify the land.

❷ What is one effect of people changing the physical environment?

_____

_____

_____

Children in History

Elfido Lopez

Elfido Lopez was born in Colorado in 1869. His family used the natural resources of the area to build a new home. The miles of wild grass fed their oxen. When he was older, Elfido learned how to cut down the wheat they grew. The river waters turned a millstone to crush their wheat into flour.

Building new homes makes more jobs for people. Then people who move into the new homes make communities grow.

People also set aside land to protect natural resources. The Cedar Point Preserve Estuary in Croatan National Forest in North Carolina is a preserved, or protected area. People are not allowed to build on preserved land.

nature preserve

People may modify the land by building roads and tunnels.

1 SUMMARIZE How do people change the physical environment? What are the consequences?

_____

_____

_____

2 Why do people **modify** the land?

_____

_____

3 Why do people set aside land so that people cannot build on it?

_____

_____

_____

Writing

Write a paragraph describing how people might modify your community in the future.

Review and Test Prep

 The Big Idea

People use natural resources to meet their needs.

Summarize the Unit

(Focus Skill) **Cause and Effect** Fill in the chart to show how people can save natural resources.

Cause

Turn off water and lights when they are not being used.

➡️

Effect

_____

_____

_____

Cause

_____

_____

_____

➡️

Effect

Resources are saved through recycling.

Use Vocabulary

Complete each sentence.

1 People can _____ old

bottles into something new.

2 People need _____, such as

water and air, to live.

3 We can make our resources last longer

by using _____.

4 When people cut down trees,

they _____, or change, the

physical environment.

5 People use boats, trains, automobiles, and

airplanes for _____.

Word Bank

natural
resources
   p. 141
conservation
   p. 145
recycle
   p. 145
transportation
   p. 148
modify
   p. 151

Think About It

Circle the letter of the correct answer.

6 Which of these helps people cross both land and water quickly?

    A cars

    B trains

    C airplanes

    D boats

7 Which of the following is a plant that people grow for food?

    A electricity

    B a crop

    C furniture

    D fuel

8 What makes electricity from the wind's energy?

    A a wind turbine

    B soybeans

    C an airplane

    D a dam

9 What can people use from trees?

    A wood

    B wind

    C electricity

    D coal

Answer each question in a complete sentence.

10 How does a dam use water to make energy?

_____

_____

11 What are some natural resources found under the ground?

_____

_____

Show What You Know

Writing Write a Story
Imagine that you have made a new kind of transportation. How would it work, and where would you go in it?

Activity Make a Bulletin Board
Draw two pictures of the same land. In the first, draw its physical features. In the second, draw how it has been modified to grow crops. Add your pictures to the bulletin board.

GO online To play a game that reviews the unit, join Eco in the North Carolina Adventures online or on CD.

People and the Marketplace

Produce at the State Farmers Market in Raleigh, North Carolina

Spotlight on Goals and Objectives

North Carolina Interactive Presentations

NORTH CAROLINA STANDARD COURSE OF STUDY

COMPETENCY GOAL 7 The learner will apply basic economic concepts and evaluate the use of economic resources within communities.

 # The Big Idea

How do people and communities use resources in the marketplace?

The marketplace is anywhere goods and services are bought and sold. Resources of the marketplace include money, the time and energy of workers, and the natural resources. People earn money to buy things they want and need.

Draw a picture of things you would like to buy from a store.

Reading Social Studies

Categorize and Classify

Learn

■ When you categorize and classify, you sort things into groups.

■ Decide what each group will be called.

■ Place each thing in a group.

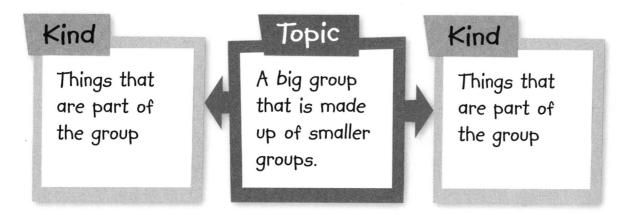

Kind

Things that are part of the group

Topic

A big group that is made up of smaller groups.

Kind

Things that are part of the group

Practice

Underline the category of exercise. Then circle the things classified as exercise.

There are many things you can do for fun. You might play sports, such as basketball and soccer. You might play with toys, such as dolls or small race cars. You might exercise by going for a walk or jumping rope.

Categorize

Classify

Apply

Read the following paragraph.

Rob and his mom shopped at the Farmers Market in Bryson City, North Carolina. They bought food, plants, toys, and drinks. They bought peppers and cucumbers. Mom chose roses and daisies for the garden. Rob bought a whistle and a puzzle. When they finished shopping, they bought drinks. Mom bought lemonade. Rob bought grape juice.

The chart below shows the things that Rob and his mom bought. What can you add to the chart?

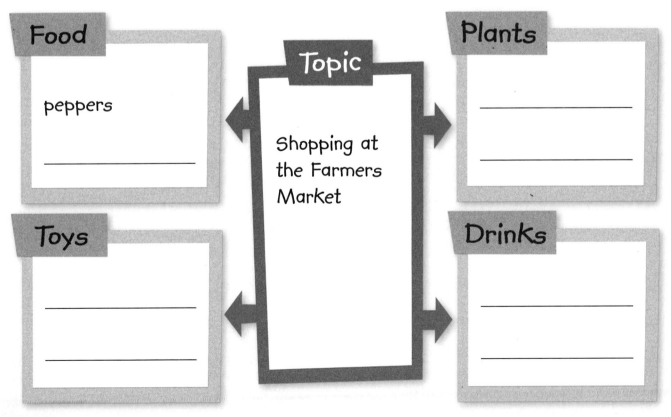

Food

peppers

_____

Plants

_____

_____

Topic

Shopping at the Farmers Market

Toys

_____

_____

Drinks

_____

_____

Producers and Consumers

Christina lives in Winston-Salem, North Carolina. She and her mom buy things downtown. They are consumers. They will buy things from producers. **What do you think you will learn about producers and consumers?**

I wood learn howa producer and consume ppltepe

NORTH CAROLINA STANDARD COURSE OF STUDY

7.01 Distinguish between producers and consumers and identify ways people are both producers and consumers

7.02 Distinguish between goods produced and services provided in communities.

Goods

Workers in a community make goods. **Goods** are things that can be bought and sold. Some goods, such as computers, are made. Other goods, such as vegetables, are grown.

Some communities are known for the goods that are made or grown there. Farms around Elizabethtown, North Carolina, grow the most blueberries in the state.

1 What are things that can be bought and sold?

goods

2 Circle the picture that shows goods being grown.

Goods

Services

Many workers in a community provide, or offer, services. A **service** is work done for others for pay. Services can be things such as haircuts and music lessons.

Doctors and nurses provide services, such as medical care. Some communities are known for their medical care. Durham, North Carolina, is known as the City of Medicine. People travel to Durham for care at its hospitals.

3 Circle three services named in the text.

4 What is Durham, North Carolina, known as?

The city of medicine

Services

Producers

In Winston-Salem, workers grow or make products to sell. A **product** is something that is made by nature or by people. Hair salons sell products such as shampoo. Workers there also provide services, such as haircuts.

A worker who grows or makes products is called a **producer**. At a bakery, bakers are producers. They make products such as bread.

TextWork

5 Underline the names of products on this page.

6 Circle the picture that shows a producer.

Consumers

Christina and her mom buy sandals at the shoe store. They also buy raisin bread at the bakery. She and her mom are consumers. A **consumer** is a person who buys and uses goods and services.

Producers can be consumers, too. The baker buys shoes at the shoe store. The person who sells shoes gets a haircut at the salon. The person who cuts hair buys bread.

TextWork

7 Look at the shoe store. Are Christina and her mom producers or consumers?

_____

Shoe Store

Bakery

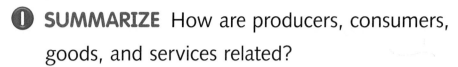

1 **SUMMARIZE** How are producers, consumers, goods, and services related?

proder are people that make goods

2 How are **goods** and **products** alike?

goods and pro are both can be made

3 How can a person be both a producer and a consumer?

a person is aproder that gorw some thing

Activity

Make a chart that shows some goods and services you buy and use.

168

People are paid money for making or selling goods or for providing services. Money that people earn is called **income**. Many people choose work that they enjoy. **What do you think you will you learn about work and income?**

_____

_____

Friendship Bracelets
For Sale

Children make and sell goods, such as bracelets, to earn income.

**NORTH CAROLINA
STANDARD COURSE OF STUDY**

7.03 Describe different types of employment and ways people earn an income.

TextWork

❶ Underline the sentence that tells what the word business means.

❷ In the pictures, circle people working for businesses.

Starting a Business

Some people have ideas for businesses of their own. A **business** is the making or selling of products or services. A person who likes to make a product might start a business. The business would sell that product. The business owner might also hire other people. Those people would help with the work. The freedom to start and run a business is called **free enterprise**.

Some people own construction or pottery businesses.

Earning Money

Children can take part in free enterprise, too. Children can wash cars or rake leaves. Children can also care for pets. Children can even sell things they make. These are all examples of free enterprise. The children who do these jobs can earn income.

People can earn income by providing services to others. There are many services people will pay others to do.

TextWork

3 Circle four ways children can take part in free enterprise.

4 What can people earn by doing things for others?

_____

Children in History

Annie Oakley

Annie Oakley's father died when she was very young. She had to learn to hunt animals for food. To earn money, she sold this food to other people in Cincinnati, Ohio. The income helped her family buy the things they needed. Later, Annie Oakley won many medals for her shooting skills.

171

Lesson 2 Review

1 **SUMMARIZE** What are some ways people earn income?

_____

_____

_____

2 What are some ways that children can take part in **free enterprise**?

_____

_____

3 Why might someone want to run a business with another person?

_____

_____

_____

Activity

Make a list of things that you like to do. Choose one that you could do to earn income.

172

People use money to pay for the goods and services they need. People also use money to pay for things they want. A **want** is something that people would like to have. **What might you learn about spending money?**

_____

_____

People spend money to pay for things they want.

NORTH CAROLINA STANDARD COURSE OF STUDY

7.04 Identify the sources and use of revenue in the community.

173

① Underline the wants named in the text.

② Circle the picture that shows someone making a choice about what to buy.

People Spend Money

People have to make choices about what they buy. First, most people buy things they need to live, such as food, clothing, and a home. Then they can buy things they want, such as books and toys.

Sometimes goods and services that people want to buy are scarce. When something is **scarce**, there is not much of it. People may have to spend more for scarce goods or buy something else.

People have to make choices about spending money.

Horizons Cineplex 10 $7.00 Student Weekend Pass

Communities Spend Money

Like people, communities also need money. Communities get money by collecting taxes. Communities spend this money to provide government services.

A community provides many government services, such as police and fire departments, roads, and parks. People in communities must decide together how to spend the community's money.

 TextWork

3️⃣ Underline four government services.

4️⃣ Circle the picture that shows a government service.

Governments use tax money to pay for new roads.

YOUR TAX DOLLARS AT WORK

1 **SUMMARIZE** What choices must people and communities make when they spend money?

_____

_____

_____

2 What happens when goods are **scarce**?

_____

_____

3 How do people decide what goods and services to buy?

_____

_____

_____

Writing

If you had ten dollars, how would you choose to spend it? Explain your answer.

People can change how they use resources. Demand and supply for goods or services may also change. **Demand** is how much consumers want to buy. **Supply** is the amount available. What will you learn about how the use of resources affects demand and supply?

_____

_____

The goods people use may change. Today, people use DVDs more than videotapes.

NORTH CAROLINA STANDARD COURSE OF STUDY

7.05 Analyze the changing uses of a community's economic resources and predict future changes.

① Underline some crops farmers grow today.

② Circle the picture that shows a farmer using his land to raise animals.

Many farms that used to grow tobacco are now used to raise cows.

Growing New Crops

At one time, North Carolina's biggest crop was tobacco. The demand for tobacco has become less over time. Today, not as many farms grow tobacco.

Farmers in North Carolina found new crops to grow. The state government helped teach farmers how to grow different crops. Some farmers grow soybeans, cabbages, or sweet potatoes. Others use the land to raise cows, pigs, or turkeys.

Finding New Jobs

The crops grown in North Carolina have changed. Some people who grew tobacco had to change their jobs. Some of them grow new crops. The state government pays for other farmers to learn to do new jobs.

In the future, the farmers of North Carolina will continue changing. They will find new ways to use the land.

 **TextWork**

❸ Circle the sentence that tells why some people in North Carolina had to change jobs.

❹ Underline the sentence that describes what farmers will do in the future.

1 **SUMMARIZE** What happens when we change how we use our resources?

_____

_____

_____

2 How are **supply** and **demand** related?

_____

_____

_____

3 Why will producers make less of a product if there is less demand for it?

_____

_____

_____

Writing

Imagine that you have a farm in North Carolina. How will you use your land?

Review and Test Prep

💡 The Big Idea

People and communities use resources in the marketplace.

Summarize the Unit

⭐(Focus Skill) **Categorize and Classify** Fill in the chart to show the parts of a marketplace.

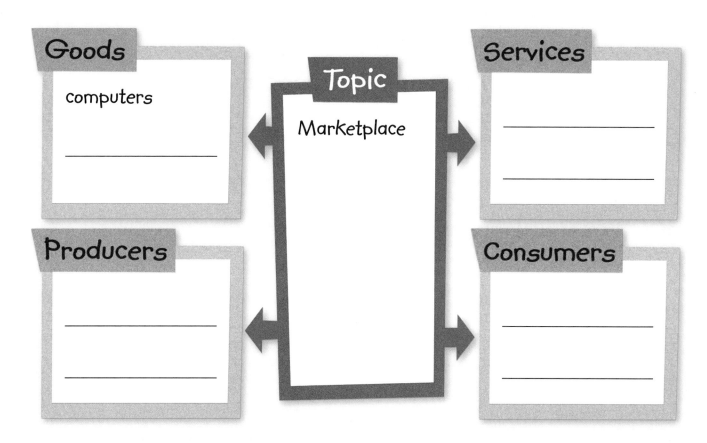

Goods

computers

_____

Topic

Marketplace

Services

_____

_____

Producers

_____

_____

Consumers

_____

_____

Use Vocabulary

Write the word under its meaning.

Word Bank

goods
  p. 164
consumer
  p. 167
business
  p. 170
want
  p. 173
supply
  p. 177

① the amount of products or services that businesses provide

_____

② something that people would like to have

_____

③ a person who buys and uses goods and services

_____

④ the making or selling of products or services

_____

⑤ things that can be bought and sold

_____

Think About It

Circle the letter of the correct answer.

6 Who helped teach farmers how to do new jobs?

    A doctors and nurses

    B business owners

    C consumers

    D the state government

7 What is a reason many people have for choosing their work?

    A It is work they enjoy.

    B They need help with the work.

    C There are many services people will pay others to do.

    D It is work they do not enjoy.

8 What is work that is done for others for pay?

    A producer

    B consumer

    C a service

    D free enterprise

9 What are children taking part in by washing cars, raking leaves, and caring for pets to earn income?

    A goods

    B free enterprise

    C products

    D government services

Answer each question in a complete sentence.

⑩ How do communities pay for government services?

_____

_____

⑪ What are some ways farmers in North Carolina use their land?

_____

_____

Show What You Know

Writing Write a Report
Think of all the goods you and your family use in your daily life. How would your life be different if you had to make all the goods you needed and wanted?

Activity Design an Ad
Think of something to sell. Why might people want to buy it? Draw an ad to sell your item. Use details to describe the item.

GO online To play a game that reviews the unit, join Eco in the North Carolina Adventures online or on CD.

Technology and Our World

A space shuttle is launched at Kennedy Space Center in Cape Canaveral, Florida

Spotlight on Goals and Objectives

North Carolina Interactive Presentations

NORTH CAROLINA STANDARD COURSE OF STUDY

COMPETENCY GOAL 8 The learner will recognize how technology is used at home, school, and in the community.

 # The Big Idea

How do people use technology in their daily lives?

People use technology in many different ways. Technology helps people in the ways they clean their homes and make meals. Technology helps people at school in the ways they learn. People also use technology for transportation and communication.

Draw a picture of a kind of technology you use.

Draw Conclusions

Learn

■ A conclusion is something you figure out.

■ Think about what you already know. Remember the new facts you learn.

■ Combine new facts with the facts you already know to draw a conclusion.

What You Learn

New facts you learn

What You Know

Information you already know

Conclusion

What conclusion can you draw from reading the paragraph?

Practice

Underline the conclusion sentence in the paragraph below.

Long ago, people had only radios for entertainment. Today, people listen to the radio, go to the movies, and watch television. The things people do for fun have changed over time.

Fact

Apply

Read the following paragraph.

Long ago, farmers planted and harvested their crops by hand. It took many workers to do all the jobs that needed to be done. Over time, people used technology to make new tools for farming. With the new tools, farmers could plant and harvest more crops faster.

What facts can you add to the chart?
What conclusion can you draw?

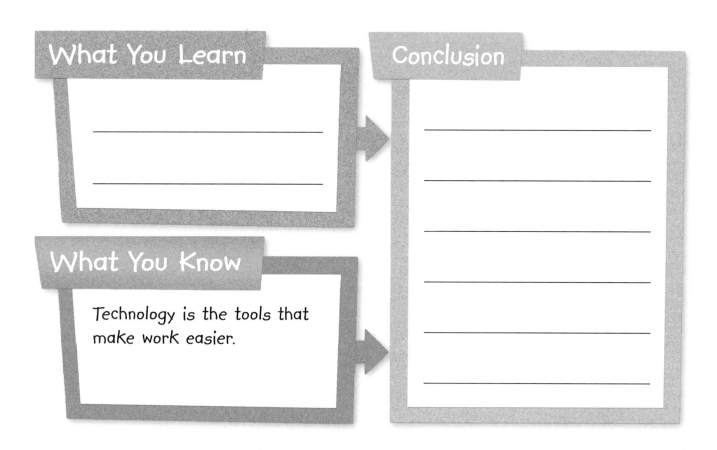

What You Learn
_____
_____

What You Know
Technology is the tools that make work easier.

Conclusion
_____
_____
_____
_____
_____
_____

Using Technology

Lesson 1

People use technology almost every day. **Technology** is all of the tools we use to make our lives easier. People use technology in transportation, in communication, at home, at school, and at work. **What will you learn about technology?**

_____

_____

Many farmers use technology to grow crops.

NORTH CAROLINA STANDARD COURSE OF STUDY

8.01 Identify uses of technology in communities.

8.02 Explain how technology has affected the world in which we live.

189

1 Underline the sentence that describes an <u>invention</u>.

2 Circle the sentence that tells what made transportation faster and easier in the late 1800s.

Transportation

New inventions change technology. An **invention** is something that has not been made before.

Automobiles were invented in the late 1800s. Since then, transportation has been faster and easier. The airplane was invented in the early 1900s. Today, people can travel long distances quickly. Some people can even travel into space!

Biography

Citizenship

Charles Moss Duke, Jr.

Charles Moss Duke, Jr., was born in Charlotte, North Carolina. He always wanted to serve his country. He learned to fly jets in the Air Force. Later, he became an astronaut. In 1972, Duke flew on the Apollo 16 lunar mission. He spent more than 71 minutes on the moon, setting a record. His team used NASA technology to explore the moon.

Communication

Communication is the sharing of ideas and information. People can use technology to communicate.

Liz's grandparents live in China. China is far away, but Liz's family members can still communicate with each other. Technology, such as the telephone and e-mail, connects people all over the world. E-mail is an electronic message sent through the Internet.

TextWork

3 Underline the sentence that describes communication.

4 Name two kinds of technology used for communication.

_____

_____

5 Circle the examples of inventions for the home.

6 Circle the picture of a child using technology at school.

Technology at Home and at School

At home, refrigerators and washing machines are inventions that make our lives easier. Toasters, vacuum cleaners, and lightbulbs are other inventions we use at home.

Many people use computers in their homes to make their lives easier. At school, many children learn with the help of computers.

Computer learning games help children study.

Farming Tools

Technology at Work

People also use technology at work. Businesses use computers to work faster and to store information.

Farmers use technology to help them grow their crops. Better tools help farmers do their work faster. Discs break up soil before seeds are planted. Cultivators loosen soil around roots of plants. Harvesters cut wheat and take out the kernels.

TextWork

7 Underline the sentence that tells how technology helps businesses.

8 Circle the farming tools shown in the pictures below.

Disc   Cultivator   Harvester

Lesson 1 Review

① **SUMMARIZE** How has technology changed the world in which we live?

_____

_____

_____

② How did the **invention** of the automobile change transportation?

_____

_____

③ Why do you think people invent new things?

_____

_____

_____

Writing

List the kinds of technology you use each day. Include examples of communication and transportation that you use at home and at school.

Using Charts and Graphs

Some information can be easier to understand in a chart or graph. Tables and flowcharts are two kinds of charts. Picture graphs and bar graphs are two kinds of graphs. **What will you learn about charts and graphs?**

_____

_____

Research Triangle Park, North Carolina

NORTH CAROLINA STANDARD COURSE OF STUDY

8.03 Interpret data on charts and graphs and make predictions.

Using a Table

A **table** organizes information in rows and columns. It can help you remember information. The title tells what the table is about. The column labels tell the kinds of information you will see.

Put your finger on the first square of a row. Then read the information in each square in that row.

TextWork

1 Which parts of a table tell the kind of information it shows?

_____

_____

2 In the table, circle the inventor of bifocal glasses.

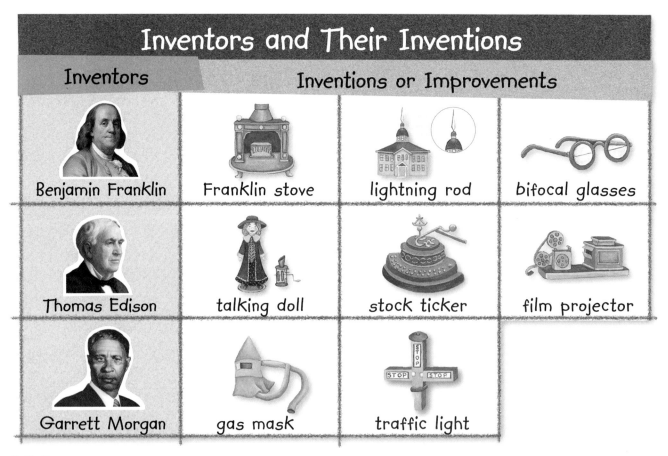

Inventors and Their Inventions

Inventors	Inventions or Improvements		
Benjamin Franklin	Franklin stove	lightning rod	bifocal glasses
Thomas Edison	talking doll	stock ticker	film projector
Garrett Morgan	gas mask	traffic light	

Using a Flowchart

A **flowchart** shows the steps needed to make or do something. The title tells what it is about. Each picture and its sentence tell about a step. The arrows show the order of the steps.

Look at the flowchart about how baseball bats are made. What is the first step? Move your finger along the arrows to see the next steps. What happens after the bats are made?

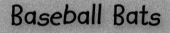
Baseball Bats

① Trees are cut down to get wood.

② The bats are made at a factory.

③ The bats are taken to stores.

④ The bats are sold at stores.

197

5 Underline the sentence that describes what the graph's key shows.

6 Did Keith's family use more water to wash dishes or to take showers?

_____

Using a Picture Graph

A **picture graph** uses pictures to show numbers of things. This picture graph shows how much water Keith's family uses in one day. The key shows what each water drop stands for.

How many water drops are next to the toothbrush? Since one water drop equals five gallons, Keith's family used five gallons of water for brushing teeth.

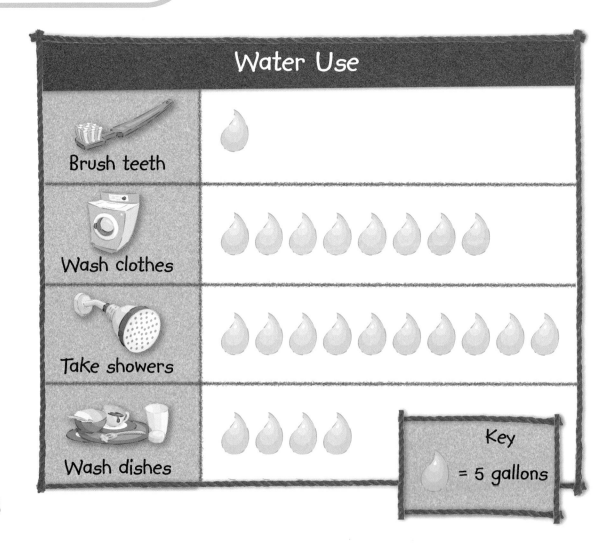

Water Use

Brush teeth	💧
Wash clothes	💧💧💧💧💧💧💧💧
Take showers	💧💧💧💧💧💧💧💧💧💧
Wash dishes	💧💧💧💧

Key
💧 = 5 gallons

Using a Bar Graph

A **bar graph** uses bars to show numbers of things. The title tells what it shows. Each bar stands for a different group. You read some bar graphs from left to right and others from bottom to top.

Find out how many dogs were groomed on Tuesday. Look at the row for that day. Move your finger to the last colored square. Move your finger down to the number. This tells you how many dogs were groomed on Tuesday.

TextWork

7 Circle the ways a bar graph can be read.

8 Six dogs were groomed on Friday. Color the correct number of squares on the bar graph.

Dogs Groomed at the Pet Palace

	0	1	2	3	4	5	6	7
Monday								
Tuesday								
Wednesday								
Thursday								
Friday								

1 **SUMMARIZE** How can you use charts and graphs to organize and understand information?

_____

_____

_____

2 How are a **picture graph** and **bar graph** alike? How are they different?

_____

_____

3 Look at the flowchart on page 197. What do you think the boy and his father will do with the baseball bat?

_____

_____

Activity

Make a bar graph. Show different kinds of pets and the number of classmates who have each kind.

Review and Test Prep

 The Big Idea

People use technology in their daily lives.

Summarize the Unit

(Focus Skill) **Draw Conclusions** Fill in the chart to show how technology will be used in the future.

What You Learn

_____

_____

_____

Conclusion

_____

_____

_____

_____

_____

_____

_____

_____

What You Know

People use technology in communication and transportation.

Use Vocabulary

Fill in the blanks with the correct words.

Mr. Matthews likes to make

1 _____, or things that have

not been made before. When he wants

to invent something, Mr. Matthews

thinks about **2** _____, or all

of the tools we use to make our lives easier.

He also thinks about the kinds of new technology

people might need. Mr. Matthews uses a

3 _____ to organize his ideas. He

decides to make a new telephone that people can

use for **4** _____. Then he uses a

5 _____ to show the steps he will

use to make his invention.

Word Bank

technology
   p. 189
inventions
   p. 190
communication
   p. 191
table
   p. 196
flowchart
   p. 197

202

Think About It

Circle the letter of the correct answer.

6 What is an electronic message sent through the Internet called?

    A an e-mail

    B a refrigerator

    C an airplane

    D an invention

7 Look at the picture graph on page 198. Which key symbol was used to show how much water Keith's family used?

    A a toothbrush

    B a water drop

    C a washing machine

    D a shower head

8 Which is not a farming tool?

    A a harvester

    B a cultivator

    C a disc

    D a toaster

9 Look at the table on page 196. Which invention or improvement did Thomas Edison make?

    A the Franklin stove

    B a gas mask

    C a talking doll

    D bifocal glasses

Answer each question in a complete sentence.

10 Why do you think people want to use technology, such as e-mail, to communicate?

_____

_____

11 Why might you choose to show information in a chart or a graph?

_____

_____

_____

Show What You Know

Writing Write About Inventions
Choose an invention from the table on page 196. Tell how life would be different if that invention had not been made.

Activity Create a Flowchart
Create a flowchart that shows the steps for something you do every day. Use the flowchart on page 197 as a model.

GO online To play a game that reviews the unit, join Eco in the North Carolina Adventures online or on CD.

For Your Reference

Glossary

R2

Index

R8

GLOSSARY

INDEX

R1

Glossary

The Glossary has important words and their definitions. They are listed in alphabetical (ABC) order. The definition is the meaning of the word. The page number at the end tells you where the word is first defined.

A

absolute location

The exact location of a place. p. 116

ancestor

A family member who lived long ago. p. 65

B

ballot

A list of all the choices for voting. p. 39

bar graph

A graph that uses bars to show numbers of things. p. 199

bay

A smaller body of water that is partly surrounded by land. p. 130

border

A line on a map that shows where a state or country ends. p. 18

business

The making or selling of products or services. p. 170

C

cape

A point of land that sticks out into water. p. 130

cardinal directions

The directions of north, south, east, and west. p. 19

change

What happens when something becomes different. p. 91

citizen

A person who lives in and belongs to a community. p. 5

climate

The kind of weather a place has over a long time. p. 123

coast

The part of the land that touches the ocean. p. 121

communication

The sharing of ideas and information. p. 191

community

A group of people who work or play together. p. 5

compass rose

The symbol on a map that shows directions. p. 19

consequence

What happens because of what a person does. p. 15

conservation

The saving of resources to make them last longer. p. 145

constitution

A written set of laws. p. 45

consumer

A person who buys and uses goods and services. p. 167

continent

One of the seven main land areas on Earth. p. 14

council

A group of people that makes decisions for the community. p. 32

crop

A plant people grow for food or for other needs. p. 144

culture

A group's ways of life. p. 63

custom

A way of doing something. p. 69

demand

How much consumers want to buy goods and services. p. 177

diversity

Different ideas and ways of living. p. 77

election

A time when people vote for their leaders. p. 37

environment

All the things around us. p. 95

flowchart

A chart that shows the steps needed to make or do something. p. 197

folktale

A story passed on over time. p. 68

Glossary ■ **R3**

free enterprise

The freedom to start and run a business. p. 170

freedom

The right to make your own choices. p. 44

fuel

Something that can be burned for heat or energy. p. 144

future

The time yet to come. p. 92

geographer

A person who studies geography. p. III

geography

The study of Earth and its people. p. III

globe

A model of Earth. p. I4

goods

Things that can be bought and sold. p. I64

government

A group of citizens that runs a community. p. 3I

government service

A service that a government provides for its citizens. p. 47

heritage

The culture that is passed down from family to family. p. 64

hero

A person who has done something brave or important. p. 7I

history

The study of things that took place in the past. p. 9I

holiday

A day when people celebrate culture, events, or heroes. p. 7I

immigrant

A person who comes from another place to live in a country. p. 65

income

The money people earn for the work they do. p. I69

independence

The freedom of people to choose their own government. p. 73

inset map

A smaller map within a larger one. p. I8

invention

Something that has not been made before. p. 190

island

A landform with water all around it. p. 121

judge

The person in charge of a court. p. 32

landform

A kind of land with a special shape. p. 119

language

The words or signs people use to communicate. p. 63

law

A rule that people in a community must follow. p. 32

map

A flat drawing that shows where places are. p. 14

map grid

A set of lines that divides a map into columns and rows of squares. p. 117

map key

The part of a map that shows what the symbols mean. p. 19

map symbol

A small picture or shape on a map that stands for a real thing. p. 17

map title

The title that tells what the map shows. p. 17

mayor

The leader of a town or city. p. 32

modify

To change something. p. 151

mountain

A very high hill. p. 120

natural resource

Something found in nature. p. 141

ocean
A very large body of water. p. 14

participate
To take part. p. 27

past
The time before now. p. 92

peninsula
Land that has water around it on all sides but one. p. 121

physical features
Features of a place that include land, water, climate, and plant life. p. 125

picture graph
A graph that uses pictures to show numbers of things. p. 198

pollution
Anything that makes the air, water, or land dirty. p. 97

present
The time right now. p. 92

producer
A worker who grows or makes products. p. 166

product
Something that is made by nature or by people. p. 166

recycle
To use the materials in old things to make new things. p. 145

region
An area of land with the same features. p. 125

relative location
A description of a place that tells what it is near. p. 116

religion
A set of beliefs about God or gods. p. 66

responsibility
Something that a person should take care of or do. p. 7

right
A kind of freedom that people have. p. 44

role
The part a person plays in a group or community. p. 59

rule
An instruction telling people what must or must not be done. p. 32

GLOSSARY

rural

An area often in the countryside, usually far from a city. p. 100

scarce

Hard to find because there is not much of it. p. 174

service

Work done for others for pay. p. 165

social environments

The places in which people meet to work or play in the community. p. 27

suburb

A smaller community near a city. p. 101

supply

The amount of products or services that businesses provide. p. 177

table

A chart that organizes information in rows and columns. p. 196

tax

Money paid to the government and used to pay for services. p. 49

technology

All of the tools people use to make their lives easier. p. 189

tradition

Something that is passed on from older family members to children. p. 67

transportation

The moving of things and people from place to place. p. 148

urban

In, of, or like a city. p. 101

volunteer

A person who works without pay to help others. p. 11

vote

A choice that is counted. p. 39

want

Something that people would like to have. p. 173

Index

The index tells where information about people, places, and events in this book can be found. The entries are listed in alphabetical (ABC) order. Each entry tells the pages where you can find the topic.

A

Aberdeen, North Carolina, 34
Absolute location, 116
Address, 15
African Americans, 73–74, 80
Air, 143
Alabama, 12, 137
Albemarle Sound, 109
Aloha Festivals, 71
American Indians, 96
Anansi the spider, 68
Ancestors, 65
Asheville, North Carolina, 23, 33, 95, 101
Asia, 67
Atlantic Ocean, 130
Automobiles, 149, 190
Avery County, North Carolina, 107

B

Baker, Ella Josephine, 44
Bakery, 166
Ballot, 39
Baltimore, Maryland, 1
Bar graph, 199
Barton, Clara, 79
Bastille Day (France), 73
Bay, 130
Bay St. Louis, Mississippi, 12

Bellamy, Terry, 33
Big Idea, The, 2, 19, 24, 51, 56, 83, 88, 103, 108, 133, 138, 155, 160, 181, 186, 201
Biography
　Baker, Ella Josephine, 44
　Duke, Charles Moss, Jr., 190
　Tan, Amy, 60
Black Mountains, 127
Blue Ridge Mountains, 126
Blue Ridge Parkway, 115
Blueberries, 164
Bodies of water, 122
Border, 18
Bryson City, North Carolina, 162
Buffalo, 96
Buses, 48
Bush, George W., 26
Business, 170
Buxton, North Carolina, 125

C

Cape, 130
Cape Canaveral, Florida, 185
Cape Fear, 122
Cape Hatteras Lighthouse, 125

Cardinal directions, 19, 113
Caring, 79
Categorize and Classify, 161–162, 181
Cause and Effect, 139–140, 155
Cedar Point Preserve Estuary, 153
Celebrations, 71
　celebrating heroes, 72
　celebrating independence, 73
　celebrating traditions, 74
　New Year celebrations, 75
Change, 91
　community changes, 88, 91, 93
　family changes, 92, 96
　people changes, 88
Chao, Elaine, 81
Charlotte, North Carolina, 15, 47, 129
Charts and Graphs
　bar graph, 199
　flowchart, 197
　government leaders, 32
　kinds of, 195
　picture graph, 198
　table, 192–193, 196
Children in History
　Lopez, Elfido, 152
　Oakley, Annie, 171

INDEX

Chinese New Year celebration, 75
Chowan River, 109
Cinco de Mayo, 74
Citizens, 5, 6
  differences, 60
  elections, 37–39
  government services, 47–49
  participation, 27
  responsibilities of, 2, 7
  social environments, 27
  voting, 39
City, 15
Climate, 123
Clothing, 63, 67, 174
Coast, 121
Coastal Plain region, 130–131, 140
  map, 130
Colonial Williamsburg, Virginia, 147
Communication, 191
Community, 5, 6
  changes in, 91, 93
  different kinds, 56
  diversity, 77
  elections, 37–39
  government and, 24
  leaders, 31–35
  roles, 59
  rural communities, 100
  similarities, 56
  spending money, 175
  suburban communities, 101
  urban communities, 101
Community activities, 29

Community government, 32
Community leaders, 31–35
  council members, 32, 34
  elections, 37–39
  judges, 32, 35
  mayors, 32, 33
Compare and Contrast, 109–110, 133
Compass, 113
Compass rose, 19
Consequences, 15–17, 42, 43
Conservation, 145
Constitution of United States, 25–26, 45
Consumers, 163, 167
Continents, 14, 15
Cotton, 137
Council, 32, 34, 38
Country, 15
Croatan National Forest, 153
Crops, 137, 144, 178
Cruso, North Carolina, 111
Culture, 163
  clothing, 63
  customs, 69
  folktales, 68
  food, 63, 69
  Ghana, 68
  Jewish, 66
  Korean, 65
  language, 63
  Mexican, 64, 74
  Pakistan, 67
  Russian, 66
  Spanish, 69
  tradition, 67
Customs, 69

D

Deep River, 128
Demand, 177
Desert, 110
Details, 3–4
Differences, 60
Diversity, 77
  fairness and, 78
Diwali (India), 75
Draw Conclusions, 187–188, 201
Duke, Charles Moss, Jr., 190
Durham, North Carolina, 31, 35, 129, 165

E

Earth, 113
Easley, Mike, 38
Edison, Thomas, 196
Elections, 37–39
Electricity, 143
Elizabethtown, North Carolina, 164
E-mail, 191
Entertainment, 187
Environment, 95.
  See also Physical environment; Social environments

F

Fairness, 78
Family
  changes in, 92
  family responsibilities, 10

INDEX

Farmers Market, 159, 162
Farming
    crops, 178–179
    goods, 164
    land use, 153
    technology, 188, 193
Finding locations, 115–117
    absolute location, 116
    relative location, 116
Fire department, 48, 49, 175
Five themes of geography, I2–I3
Flowchart, 197
Folktales, 68
Fontana Lake, 122
Food, 63, 69, 174
Forest, I10
Fort McHenry, 1
Foster children, 13
Franklin, Benjamin, 196
Free enterprise, 170
Freedom of press, 45
Freedom of religion, 45
Freedom of speech, 45
Freedoms, 44–45
French Broad River, 126
Fuel, 144
Future, 92

Generalize, 25–26, 51
Geographer, III
Geography, III
    five themes of geography, I2–I3
    geography terms, I10
    learning about places, 108

Geography Review, II–I10
Geography terms, I10
Ghana culture, 68
Globe, I4, II3
Glossary, R2–R7
Goods, 164
Government, 31
    community government, 32
    laws, 32, 43
    leadership, 31
    national government, 38
    rights and freedoms, 44–45
    rules, 32, 41
    taking part, 24
Government leaders, 31–35
    chart, 32
Government services, 47–49, 175
Governors, 38
Grace, North Carolina, 101
Grandfather Mountain Highland Games, 58
Great Smoky Mountains, 121, 126
Greensboro, North Carolina, 87, 129
Greer, Pedro Jose, Jr., 81
Groups, 28
Gulf, I10, 122

Hair salon, 166
Hanami (Japan), 74
Haw River, 128

Hawaii, 71
Helping, 81
Heritage, 64
Heroes, 71
    holidays celebrating heroes, 72
Hickory, North Carolina, 13
High Rock Lake, 128
Highland Games, 58
Hill, I10
History, 91
Holidays, 71
    celebrating heroes, 72
    celebrating independence, 73
Homes, 151
Hudson, Orlando, Jr., 35
Human–environment interactions, I3
Hurricane Katrina, 12
Hyde County, 130–131

Immigrants, 65
Income, 169
    children earning money, 171
Independence, 73
Independence Day, 73
Index, R8–R13
India, 75
Inset map, I8
Internet, 191
Inventions, 190, 196
    table, 196
Islam, 67
Island, I10, 121
Israel, 80

J

Japan, 74
Jewish culture, 66, 75, 80
Jobs, 61, 179, 193
  income, 169
Judges, 32, 35
Juneteenth, 73

K

Kennedy Space Center, 185
King, Dr. Martin Luther, Jr., 72
Koontz, Elizabeth Duncan, 80
Korean culture, 65
Kwanzaa, 74

L

Lake, 110, 122
Lake Norman, 128
Landforms, 119, 120–121, 149
Language, 63
Laws, 32, 43
Leaders, 31–35, 37–39
Linville, North Carolina, 58
Litter, 29
Little Tennessee River, 126
Location, 12, 18
  absolute location, 116
  relative location, 116
Lopez, Elfido, 152
Louisiana, 12
Louisville, Kentucky, 55

M

Maal Hijra, 75
Mail delivery, 48
Main Idea and Details, 3–4, 19
Manteo, North Carolina, 110
Map grid, 117
Map key, 19
Map symbol, 17, 19
Map title, 17
Maps, 14
  Coastal Plain region, 130
  definition, 14
  inset maps, 18
  kinds of maps, 112
  Mountain region, 126
  neighborhood map, 17
  Piedmont region, 128
  population of North Carolina, 101
  reading maps, 18
  of United States, 19, 112
  world map, 14
Marietta, Ohio, 92–93
Markets, 159, 160
Mayors, 32, 33, 38
Medical care, 165
Meir, Golda, 80
Memorial Day, 72
Mexican culture, 64, 74
Mississippi, 12
Mississippi River, 126
Modify, 151
Modifying land, 151–153
Money
  children earning money, 171
  marketplace and, 160
  spending money, 173–175
Morgan, Garrett, 196
Mother Teresa, 79
Mount Mitchell, 126
Mountain region, 126–127, 140
  map, 126
Mountains, 110, 120, 149
Movement, 13
  transportation, 48, 148–149, 190
Muslim, 75

N

National Heroes Day (Philippines), 72
Natural resources, 141–145
  air, 143
  conservation, 145
  fuel, 144
  soil, 144
  trees, 143, 152
  using natural resources, 138
  water, 142
Neighborhood, 16, 17
  suburban neighborhoods, 101
Neighborhood map, 17
New Bern, North Carolina, 15, 89
New Year celebration, 75
Nobel Prize, 77
North Carolina
  climate, 123
  community leaders, 32–35

INDEX

North Carolina (continued)
crops, 178–179
goods, 164, 178
governor, 38
Hurricane Katrina volunteers, 12
map of, 126, 128, 130
medical care, 165
producers, 166
regions, 125–131
services, 165
Special Olympics, 4
state capital, 89
state seal, 38

Oakley, Annie, 171
Oceans, 14, 110, 130
Outer Banks, 97, 121

 (P)

Pakistan, 67
Participate, 27
Past, 92
Pee Dee River, 109
Peninsula, 110, 121
Philippines, 72
Physical environment, 13, 95, 147
long ago environment, 93, 96
modifying land, 151–153
pollution, 97

Physical features, 125
Picture graph, 198
Piedmont region, 128–129, 140
map, 128
Place, 12
Plain, 110
Police department, 43, 48, 49, 175
Pollution, 97
Pottery, 170
Present, 92
President, 38
Presidents' Day, 72
Press, 45
Producers, 166, 167
Products, 166

(R)

Raleigh, North Carolina, 89, 91, 129, 159
Reading social studies skills
Categorize and Classify, 161–162, 181
Cause and Effect, 139–140, 155
Compare and Contrast, 109–110, 133
Draw Conclusions, 187–188, 201
Generalize, 25–26, 51
Main Idea and Details, 3–4, 19
Recall and Retell, 57–58, 83
Sequence, 89–90, 103

Recall and Retell, 57–58, 83
Recycling, 145
Red Cross, 79
Regions, 13, 125
Coastal Plain region, 130–131, 140
Mountain region, 126–127, 140
physical features, 125
Piedmont region, 128–129, 140
Relative location, 116
Religion, 66, 67, 75
Religious freedom, 45
Research Triangle Park, 195
Responsibilities, 7, 9
acting responsibly, 10, 16–17
citizens and, 2, 7
helping others, 11–13
Right, 44
Rights and freedoms, 44–45
River, 110, 122
Robinson, Jackie, 78
Rocky River, 109
Roles, 59
Rosh Hashanah, 75
Rules, 32, 41, 42
Rural areas, 100
Russian culture, 66

 (S)

Scarce, 174
School activities, 28

School responsibilities, 10
School technology, 192
Scotland, 57–58
Sequence, 89–90, 103
Service, 80
Services, 165
Shannon, Donna, 34
Skiing, 107
Slavery, 73
Social environments, 27
  citizens, 27
  community activities, 29
  school activities, 28
Soil, 144
Songs, 64
South Korea, 65
Southern Pines, North Carolina, 12
Space shuttle, 185
Spanish culture, 69
Special Olympics, 4
Speech, 45
Sports, 4, 5, 60, 107
Square dancing, 55
State, 15
Suburbs, 101
Subways, 48
Sugar Mountain, North Carolina, 107
Suitcases for Kids, 13
Summer, 123

Supply, 177
Sylva, North Carolina, 110

Table, 192–193, 196
Taiwan, 81
Tan, Amy, 60
Taxes, 49, 175
Technology, 189
  communication technology, 191
  farming, 188, 193
  at home, 192
  in school, 192
  space shuttle, 185
  transportation technology, 190
  uses for, 164, 186, 189
  at work, 193
Telephone, 191
Tennessee Valley, 137
Tobacco, 178–179
Tools, 188–189
Topsail Beach, North Carolina, 97
Tradition, 67
Trains, 148
Transportation, 48, 148–149, 190
Trees, 143
Truth, Sojourner, 78

United States, 15
  holidays, 72, 73–74
  maps of, 19, 112
Urban areas, 101

Valley, 110
Volunteer, 3–4, 11–13
Vote, 39

Wants, 173
Water, 142
Waynesville, North Carolina, 100
Weather, 123
Whitewater Falls, 119
Wilmington, North Carolina, 5
Wind turbines, 143
Winston-Salem, North Carolina, 129, 163, 166
Winter, 123
Wolf Creek Dam (Kentucky), 142
Work, 61, 179, 193
  income, 169
World map, 14

INDEX